Haegue Yang

Strange Attractors

Tate St Ives

TATE

Previous page: *Sonic Intermediate – Parameters and Unknowns after Gabo* 2020
Previous page and front cover: *Sonic Intermediate – Parameters and Unknowns after Hepworth* 2020
Back cover: *Reflected Metallic Cubist Dancing Mask* 2020
Inside back cover: *Sonic Half Moon Type II – Large Light #21* 2014
This page: *Sonic Intermediate – Parameters and Unknowns after Li* 2020

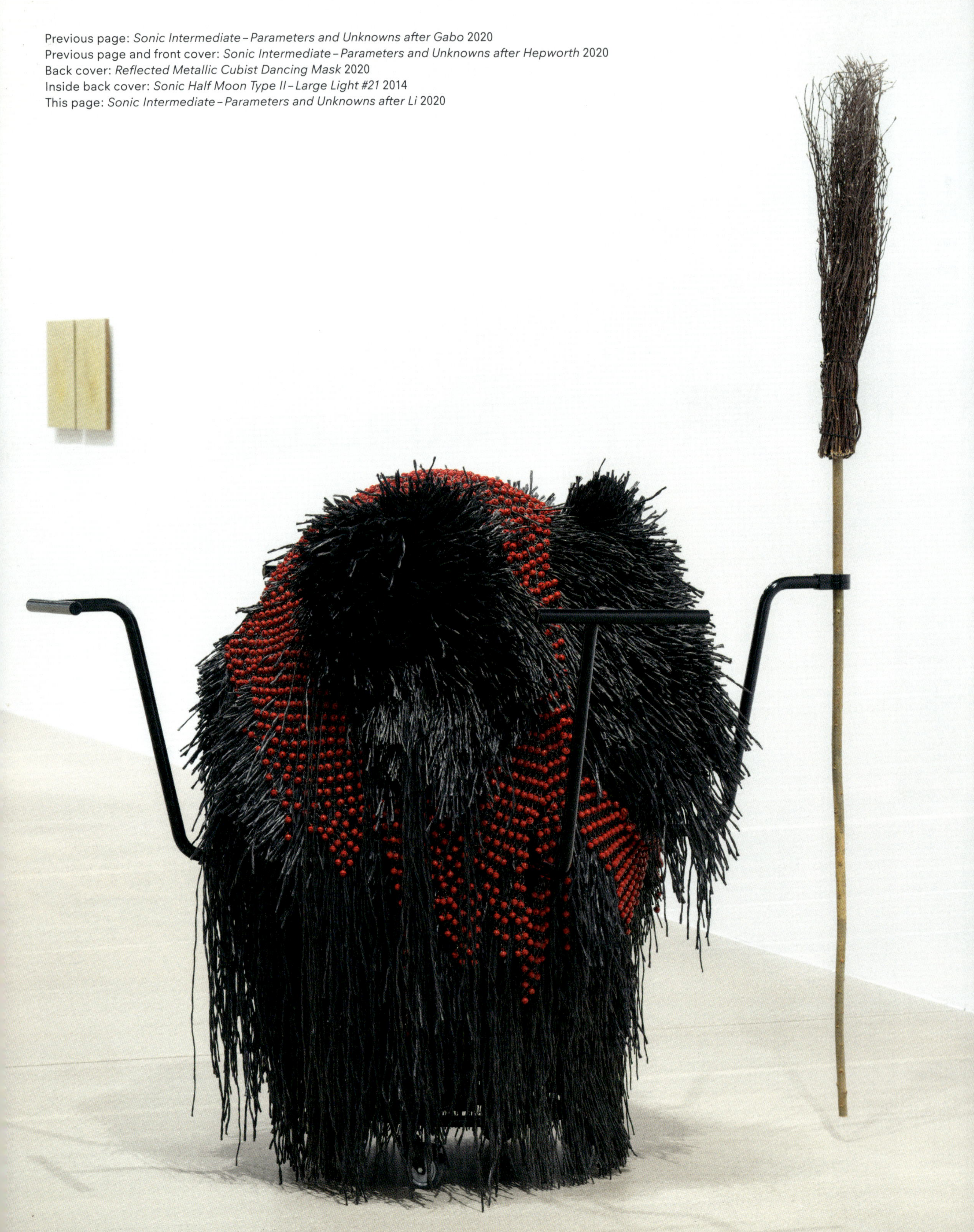

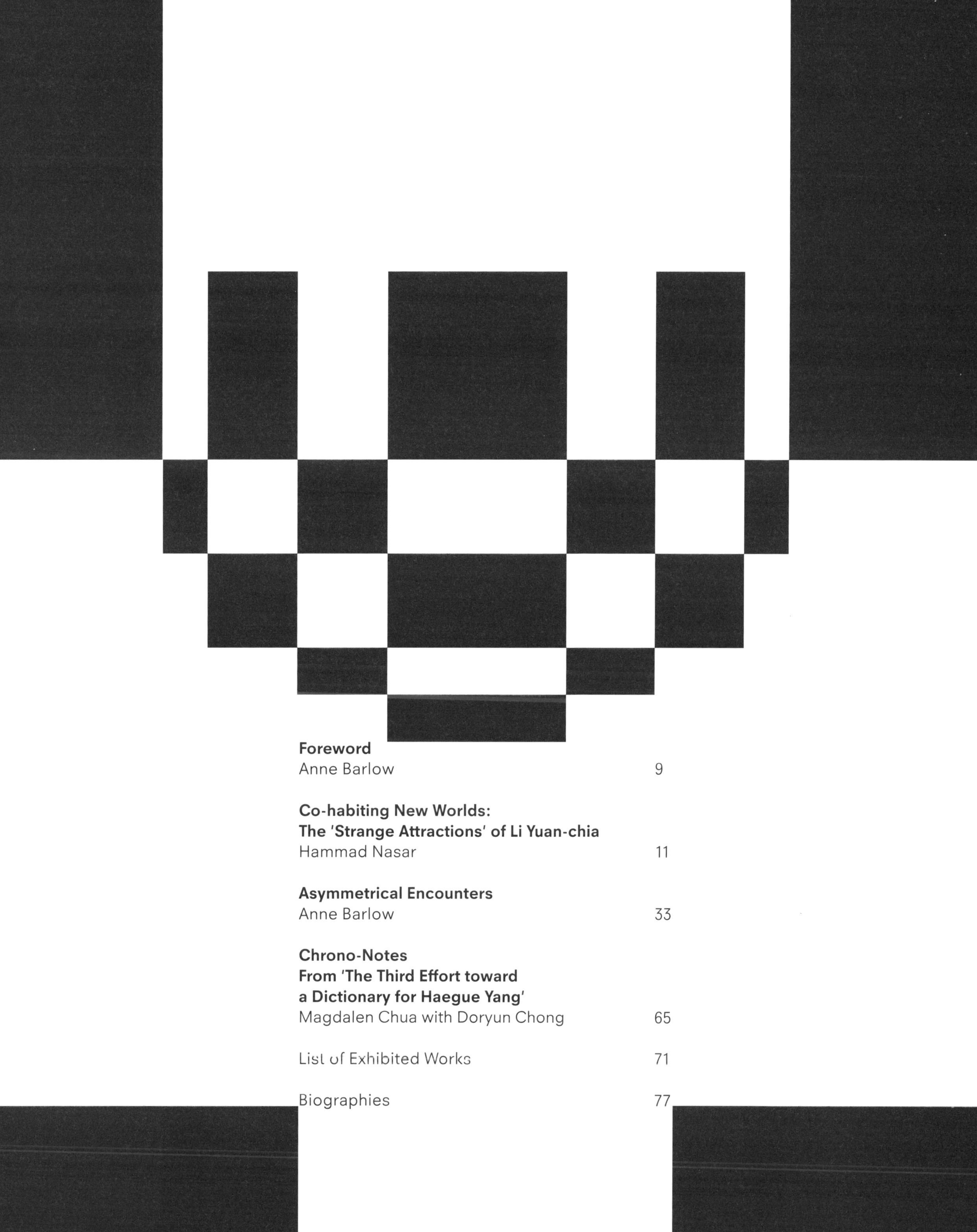

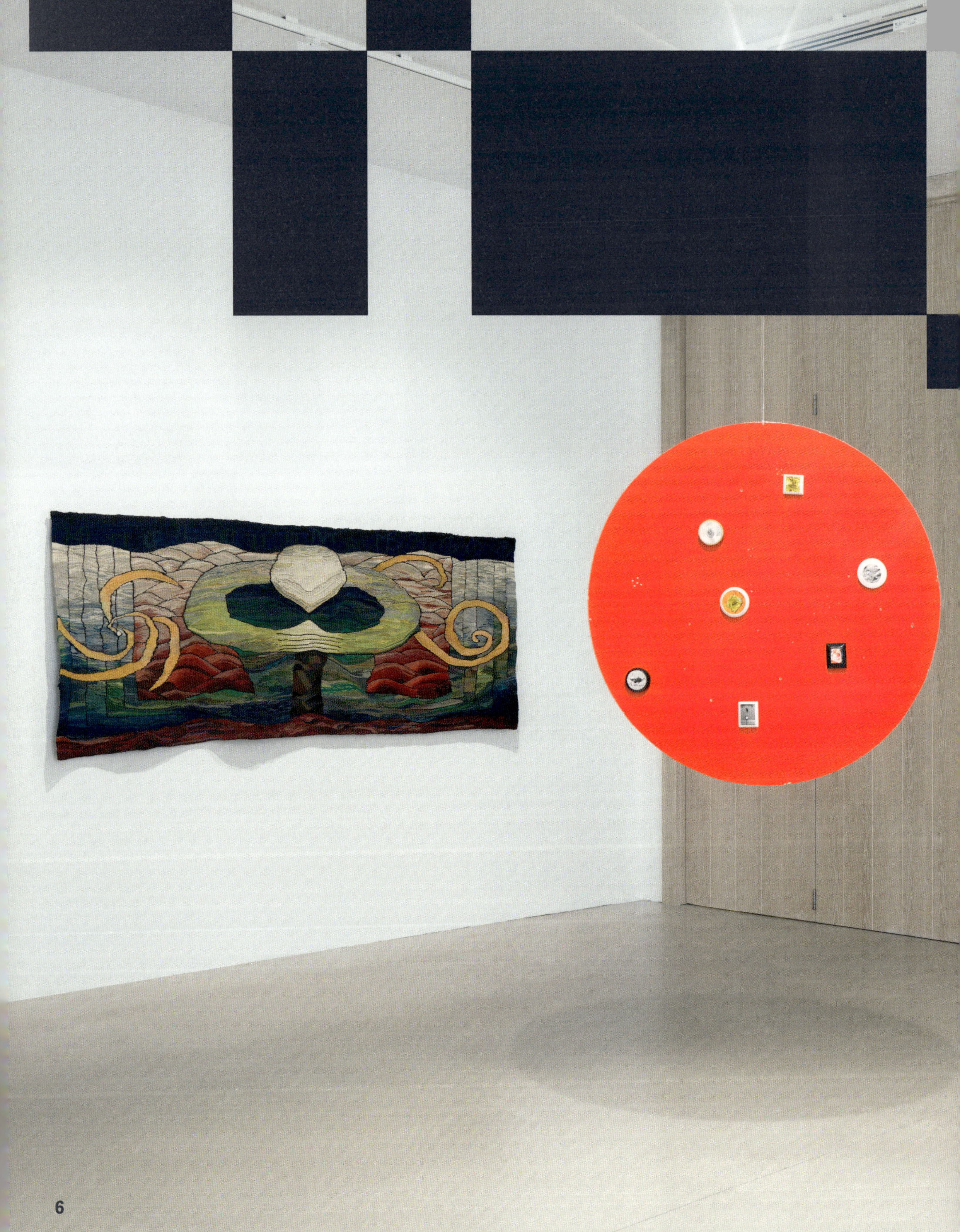

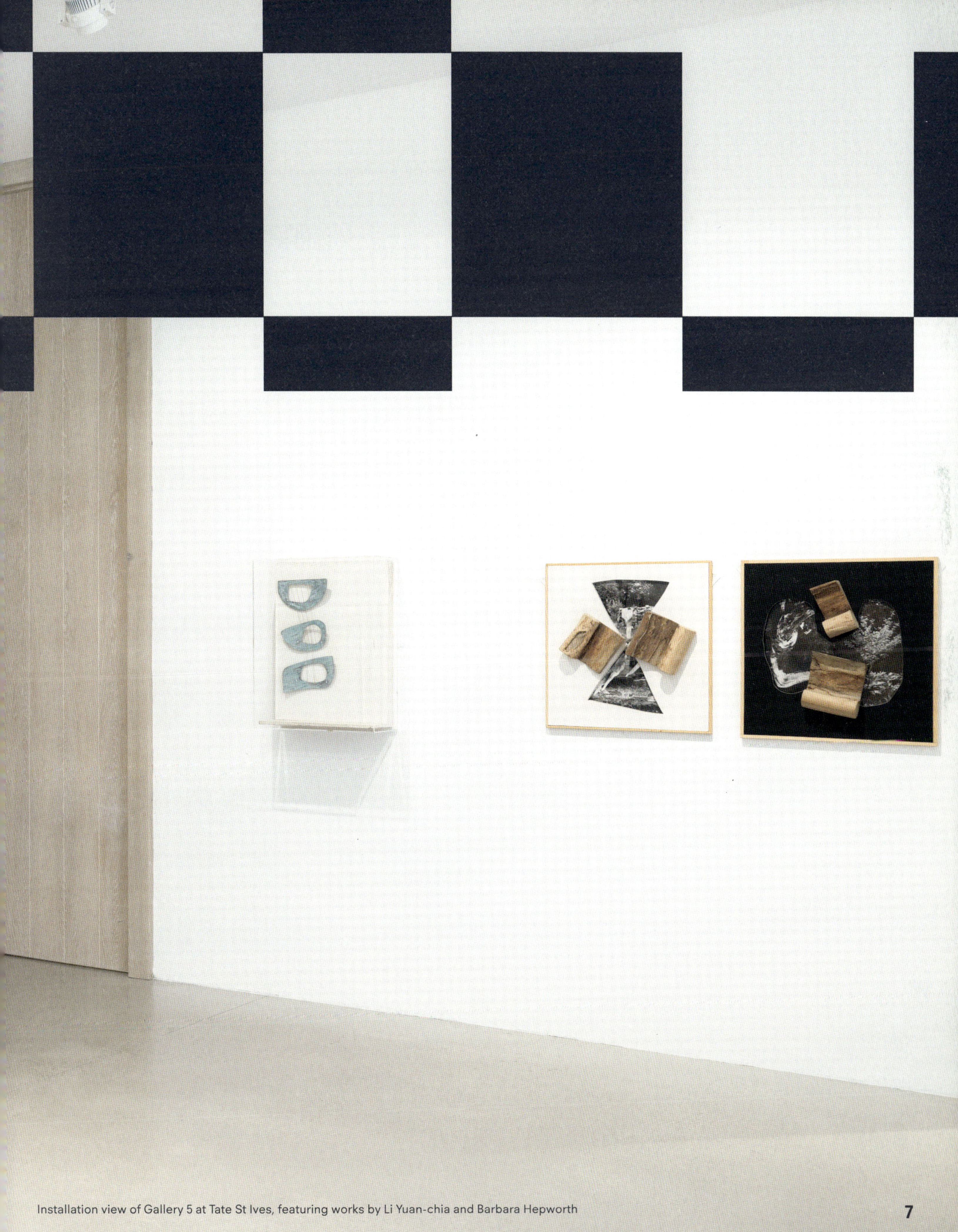

Installation view of Gallery 5 at Tate St Ives, featuring works by Li Yuan-chia and Barbara Hepworth

Li Yuan-chia
Untitled 1980s

Foreword

Haegue Yang brings together materials, theories and cultural references to make astute and surprising connections between local contexts and wider geographies and histories. In her inimitable way, she has created a unique exhibition that spans the two galleries created as part of the extension to Tate St Ives that opened in 2017 and the curved, sea-facing gallery at the core of the original building.

The exhibition begins with a display of work by three artists associated directly or indirectly with St Ives – Naum Gabo, Barbara Hepworth and Li Yuan-chia – immediately followed by a new tripartite sculpture inspired by them, made as a continuation of Yang's *Intermediates* series. Yang has also created a range of other new works for the exhibition, including a sculpture, a large-scale wallpaper, new *Trustworthies* and an installation referencing church kneeler cushions she saw in Zennor, Cornwall. These new projects are shown alongside existing works in immersive environments, creating an experience for visitors that we hope is surprising, thought-provoking and captivating.

We would like to express our warmest thanks to Liene Harms, Zarah Landes, Emmy Skensved and the rest of the team at Studio Haegue Yang for their rigorous and generous approach to making this ambitious and multi-faceted project happen. We are extremely grateful to Galerie Barbara Wien, Berlin and Galerie Chantal Crousel, Paris for their support of this exhibition, the private collectors who have generously lent to the show, and the Li Yuan-chia Foundation for graciously allowing us the opportunity to show Li's work. Our sincere thanks go to the Henry Moore Foundation and Institut für Auslandsbeziehungen for their vital support of the show, and to Kvadrat for generously providing fabric to create the translucent and iridescent surface across our sea-facing gallery window with the support of Julia Rodrigues at South into North. We would also like to express our thanks to all Tate staff who have made this project possible, especially Giles Jackson, Sally Noall, Helen Bent, Sara Matson and the Conservation and Technical teams.

This publication is both a document of the exhibition and an expansion of the ideas that punctuate it, bringing together installation photography and new texts on Haegue Yang. Hammad Nasar's reflection on Yang's interest in the artist Li Yuan-chia is followed by an introduction to the central themes of the exhibition and the new works created by Yang, as well as a text by Magdalen Chua and Doryun Chong that takes the form of a timeline of events and people that have been significant in the development of Yang's practice. We are extremely grateful to the writers for their insightful contributions, to Studio Manuel Raeder for their dynamic and responsive approach to the design of this book, and to Neil Stewart for his skilful editing of its content.

Above all, we are enormously grateful to Haegue Yang for sharing her singular and extraordinary artistic vision of a world that is in equal parts complex, chaotic and interconnected.

Anne Barlow, Director, Tate St Ives

I4-5-68

One word to x

Because

The sun pure out from east
For its one day beginning again

I saw it

The old birds very hard it found food
For its they are child in the house

Because

I like Brampton for its make me
to love this world again

Because

From mountains to hills
From vellege to cottage
From peaply to peaply
From moonlight line altogether
for its compare an great family

Because

She all remains happy and whistle
How is pitty stoped high art of heart
You well to know great-mother painter
I well hate the clouds that hidden the sun
Kind heart as jewels worth
I well song
I well love

Li Yuan-chia
One word to x 14 May 1968
LYC Foundation, Li Yuan-chia Archive, The University of Manchester Library

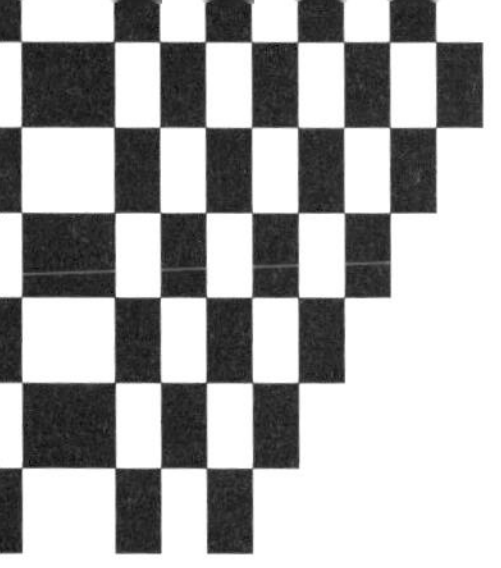

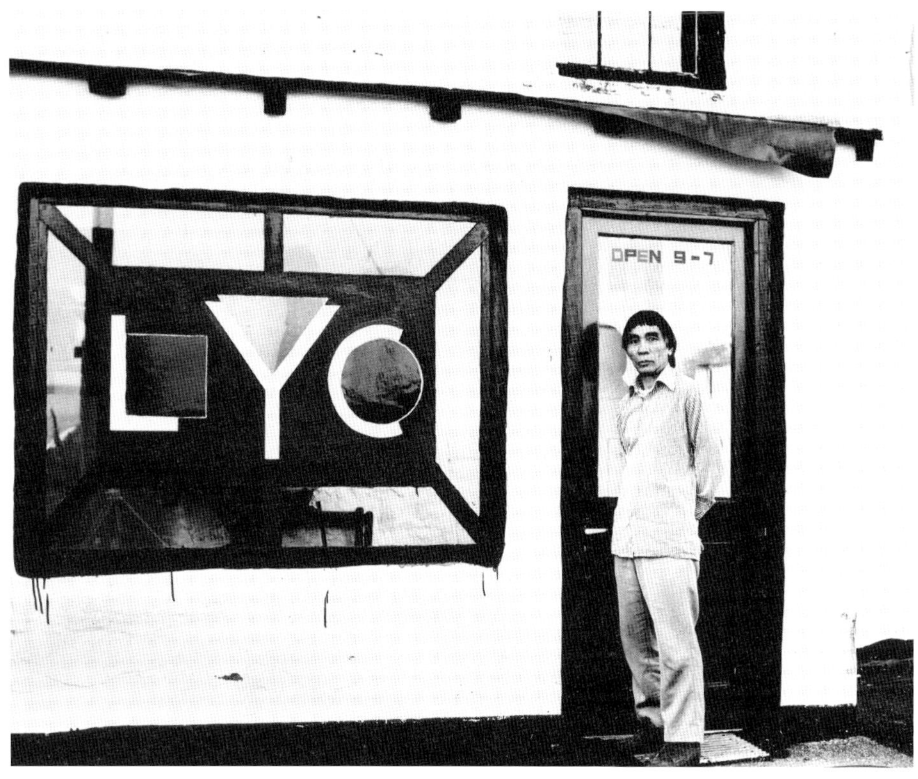

Li Yuan-chia standing at the porch of the LYC Museum & Art Gallery, featuring window designed by David Nash. LYC Foundation, Li Yuan-chia Archive, The University of Manchester Library

Co-habiting New Worlds: The 'Strange Attractions' of Li Yuan-chia

Hammad Nasar

> *I often return to the agonizing, yet compelling, lives of artists whose biographies reveal an oscillation between their engagement in art and politics.*
> Haegue Yang[1]

Audiences will enter the principal exhibition space of Haegue Yang's solo exhibition at Tate St Ives, *Strange Attractors*, through a small but varied presentation of works by artist Li Yuan-chia (1929–94), shown alongside works by Barbara Hepworth (1903–75) and Naum Gabo (1890–1977). This is doubly unusual: firstly, for an artist to frame a solo exhibition in conversation with the work of other artists; and secondly, within Yang's practice, to make her interests so plainly visible.

Who was Li? And why is his work – in particular the extraordinary LYC Museum & Art Gallery, through which he came into the orbit of the St Ives community of artists – a fruitful lens through which to consider Yang's practice?[2]

> *The fact that Li Yuan-chia has been missed by the art establishments of so many countries suggests that they have no instruments fine enough to detect a journey such as his ... crossing geographical and cultural boundaries but also those of the concepts and practices of art.*
> Guy Brett[3]

In 2014, the Taipei Fine Art Museum's expansive posthumous retrospective *View–Point: A Retrospective of Li Yuan-chia* positioned Li as the 'father of conceptual and abstract art in Taiwan', more than fifty years after he left the country.[4] Li, however, remains largely unrecognised in Britain, his home from 1966 until his death in 1994,[5] his work mostly unaccounted for in the generally circulating institutional and academic histories of art in Britain.[6]

This is at least partly due, as Guy Brett points out, to the distinctive genealogy of Li's work, which resists attempts to slot it into a singular label. He drew liberally from modernist, Zen Buddhist and Daoist practices to explore ideas of space, life and time. His interests and experiments with form were shaped by, and reflected, the zigzagged trajectories of his life. Born in Guangxi, China, Li moved first to Taiwan in 1949, where he was part of the Ton-Fan Group of artists experimenting with abstraction, then in 1962 to Bologna, where he was associated with the Punto Group of artists. An invitation to show his work at Signals

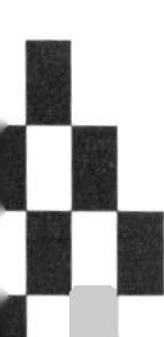

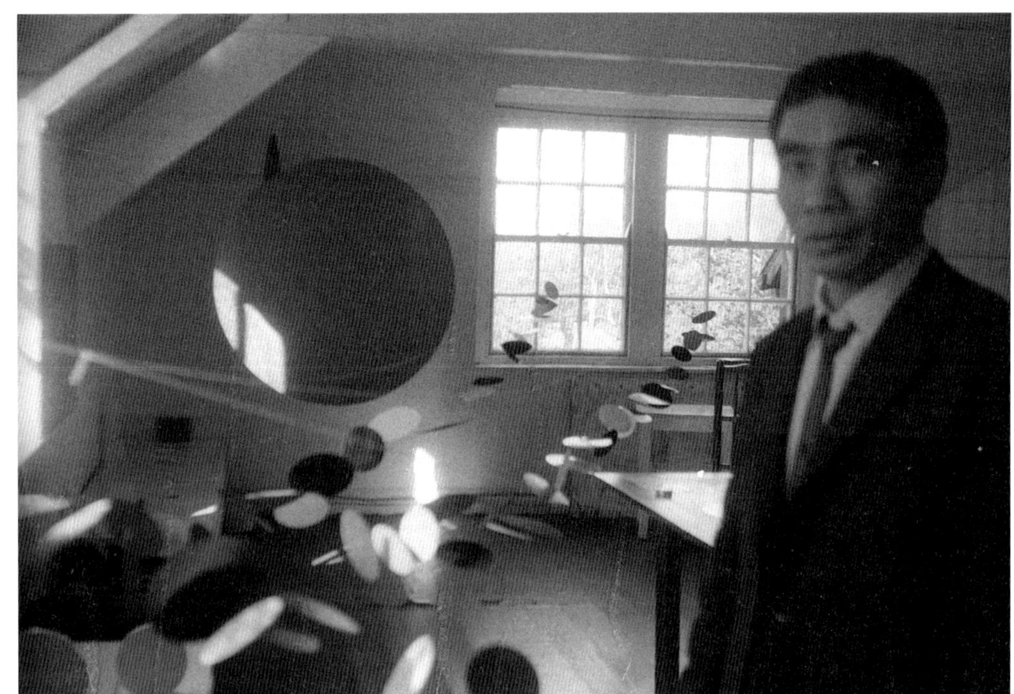

Li Yuan-chia in his studio at the LYC Museum & Art Gallery, Brampton, Cumbria, 1969. Richard Demarco Archive, University of Dundee (A.69.033)

Gallery (1965 and 1966) brought him to London. The artists he showed with at Signals and Lisson Gallery included Lygia Clark, Ken Cox, Ian Hamilton Finlay, dom sylvester houédard, Derek Jarman, David Medalla, Mira Schendel and Takis.[7] With them Li shared multiple avant-garde interests – in kinetics, participation and concrete poetry – and a questioning attitude towards the perceived boundaries between life and art.

But the London art world's regard for Li was not wholly reciprocated. On visiting his friend Nick Sawyer's family home in Cumbria for Christmas in 1967, he decided to stay in the area for the rest of his life. He settled in nearby Bankside to develop arguably his most important work – the remarkable art space he founded in the Cumbrian village of Banks, The LYC Museum & Art Gallery (LYC or LYC Museum).

Already an artist and poet, Li now became a designer-maker and curator of art and social interaction. The site's transformation from dilapidated farm buildings – acquired from his friend and neighbour, the painter Winifred Nicholson – into a hyper-active space for art was the result of Li's single-minded effort. The completed LYC Museum would host up to four new exhibitions a month, each accompanied by a catalogue that Li designed and printed, ultimately showcasing the work of more than 300 artists between 1972 and 1983. As well as St Ives artists including Winifred Nicholson, Ben Nicholson, Barbara Hepworth, Peter Lanyon and Naum Gabo, Li's eclectic exhibition programme mixed local artists (Andy Christian, Susie Honour) with totemic national figures (Paul Nash) and contemporary artists now of international renown (Lygia Clark, Andy Goldsworthy) but then barely known in Britain. Apart from galleries, the LYC had a children's art room, library, performance space, printing press, communal kitchen, and garden. It was an open space for the multiple possibilities of art, and researchers have only recently begun to explore the networks and practices that the LYC enabled.[8]

> *You can look at my work symbolically*
> *You can think of it conceptually*
> *You can play with it as a kind of toy or game*
> *Or you can appreciate it for its own beauty*
> Li Yuan-chia[9]

Haegue Yang's 'return' to 'compelling'[10] artists often takes shape as abstracted sculptural installations – part speculative fiction, part immersive participation. Interests and influences are not spelt out. So what does this unusually overt juxtaposition of Li's works with her own mean?

In keeping with Yang's practice, where the work of the imagination is foremost, I will posit three speculative propositions, advanced without any correspondence with Yang, as to what attracted her to Li's work, and what encounters she wished to set up.

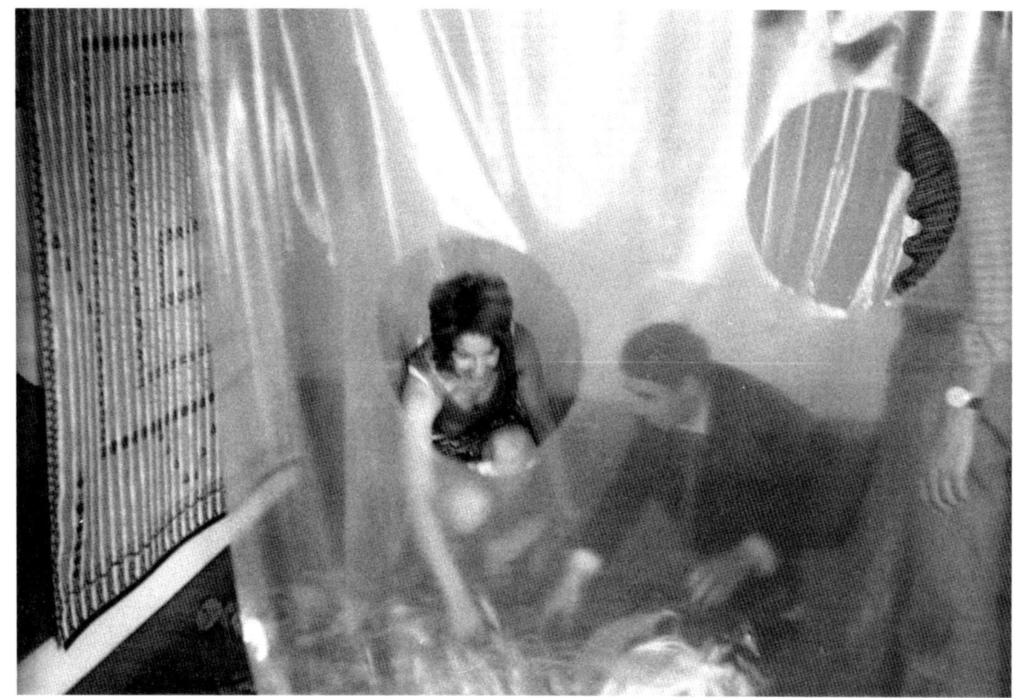

Li Yuan-chia with a group of unidentified visitors at Li Yuan-chia's studio at the LYC Museum & Art Gallery, Brampton, Cumbria, 1969. Richard Demarco Archive, University of Dundee (A.69.033)

An invitation to participate

Installation photographs of Li's 1968 experimental exhibition in Nick Sawyer's family home, Boothby, show elaborate arrangements of circular discs, many featuring movable magnetic objects. Plastic sheets, hung from the ceiling with circular holes cut in them, delineate micro-environments within the large space. One photograph from the exhibition shows a web-like installation with washing line strung across the trees in Boothby's courtyard. Several show Li encouraging his visitors to interact directly with the work.

In 1971 Li participated in *Popa at Moma: Pioneers of Part-Art* at Museum of Modern Art, Oxford alongside Lygia Clark, John Dugger, David Medalla, Hélio Oiticica and Graham Stevens. The first significant attempt in the UK to frame participatory practices (Part-Art) as an artistic tendency, *Popa at Moma* achieved notoriety when a rowdy crowd forced the show to open and close on the same evening.[11] While some artists withdrew their work, Li was happy for his to remain. This continued openness to share agency, allowing his viewers to determine the terms on which they participated, was later channelled into the functioning of the children's art room at the LYC, where both Li's art works and art materials were available for children to 'play' with. It was this participation that completed his work, and underpins his oft-repeated quote about the nature of his project: 'L.Y.C. Museum is me. L.Y.C. Museum is all of you'.[12]

This urge to share agency by inviting direct participation is also reflected in Haegue Yang's work. At Tate St Ives, her freestanding triangular structures divide space but allow people to see through; the hanging translucent fabric brings the outside in. In this exhibition, as in others, gallery attendants or facilitators act as surrogate participants, activating her moving sculptural works.

This will to movement raises questions about the nature of the work. Are the objects a different artwork when they are moved? Does their meaning change depending on how and by whom they are moved? What kinds of exhibition environments can these works live in? Can they infect this environment, or does the institutional duty to conserve impinge on the invitation to interact?

A valorisation of everyday creativity and making

Space & Freedom (2018), artist-filmmaker Helen Petts's filmic exploration of the rhythms, textures, sights and sounds of the Cumbrian landscape that inspired Li, is punctuated by sequences from archival footage showing Li at work.[13] We see him digging trenches and moving soil around by wheelbarrow, building a foundation wall and carrying buckets of water, his arms bulging from the strain. Additional footage shows him carving, sculpting or making stop motion animations. By suggesting equivalence between these activities, the film captures Li's valorisation of everyday making and living.

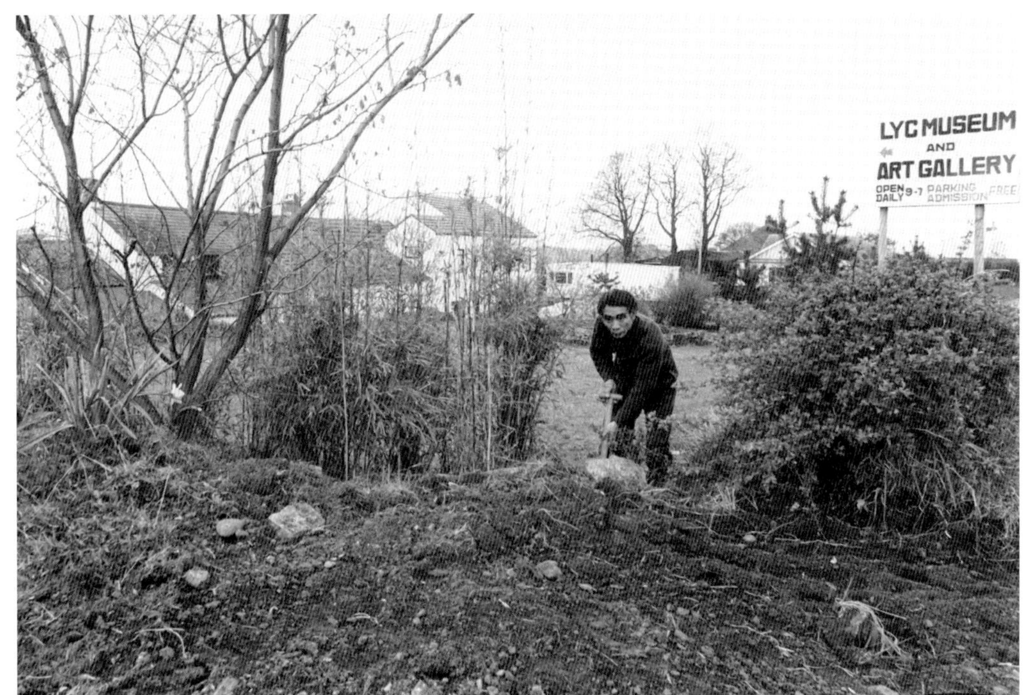

Li Yuan-chia digging outside the LYC Museum & Art Gallery LYC Foundation, Li Yuan-chia Archive, The University of Manchester Library

Similarly, Li's own remarkable series of hand-tinted photographs, taken in the grounds of the LYC after it closed, uses everyday objects (scarves, shearing scissors, a chair, a broom, an axe) and his own body as props. All aspects of his environment – natural, artistic, mass-produced or communal – fed into Li's wide-ranging creative practice.

Haegue Yang's *Sonic Intermediates – Three Differential Equations* 2020 – composite sculptures of powder-coated steel, twine and other materials – include one made after Li, the broom from one of Li's self-portraits acting as a visual baton from the everyday passed across time. Through myriad components of Yang's exhibition – the wallpaper, a shield-like sculpture on wheels, a display of small lacquer paintings, and cross-stitched cushions that reference 'church kneelers' in English parish church pews – one glimpses a common spirit at play. Hers too is a practice entirely comfortable trespassing multiple boundaries: of craft and fine art; of concept and whimsy; of seemingly parallel genealogies of practice.

The will to know | The possibility to remain unknown

> *I always wish my works to be me*
> *I always want space and freedom*
> *And so my work naturally progresses*
> *towards cosmic ideas*
> Li Yuan-chia[14]

The initial vehicle for Li's explorations was 'the Point'. Originally a spot of colour or mark on monochromatic paintings and wooden reliefs, it evolved into movable magnetised objects which he called 'toys', as well as 'photographic points' and 'poem points'. Timed to coincide with Apollo 11's mission to the moon, his *Golden Moon Show* (1969) at the Lisson Gallery allowed his points free rein, encouraging cosmological readings of his work; his articulation of the Point as 'the origin and end of creation' echoed contemporaneous scientific discussions of the Big Bang Theory, which was only widely accepted by cosmologists in the 1970s and 1980s.

Li's magnetic points were circular, square or triangular, and restricted to four colours with fixed symbolic meanings: black (origin and end), red (blood/life), gold (nobility) and white (purity). This systemic thinking is also observable in his copious use of equations in naming both his works (for example, *B+N=0* 1965) and later his exhibitions (for example, *1+3=6* (1980)) at the LYC. The aim of these seemingly eccentric formulations, like sufi poetry or Zen archery, seems to be to have no aim. For someone whose work is often so visually simple and direct, Li is paradoxically elusive.

Li Yuan-chia's art raises questions that traverse vast fields of thought. What is art? Who is it for? Who is an artist?

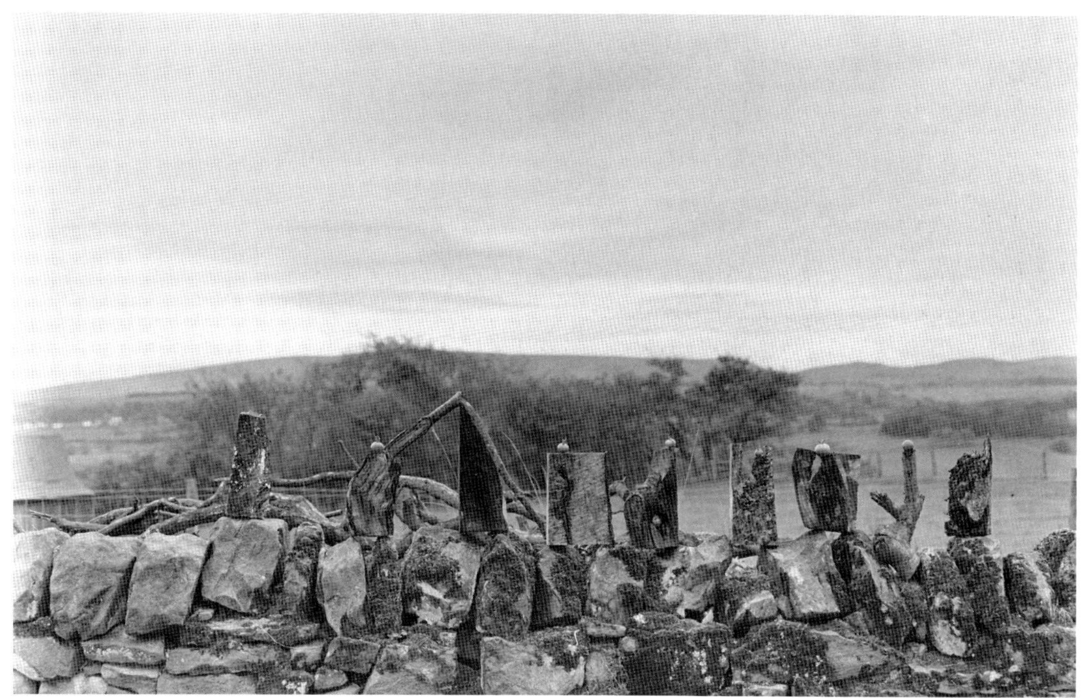

Tomatoes balanced on wooden blocks in the gardens and grounds around the LYC Museum & Art Gallery
LYC Foundation, Li Yuan-chia Archive, The University of Manchester Library

Can art help us make sense of our place in the world? How can it help us live better lives?

Li wrote often about these questions, in prose and poems. But like his self-portraits, his writings conceal as much as they reveal. They offer if not quite opacity, then translucence – shiny enough for those engaging with his work to catch their own reflection.

Haegue Yang's work shares this quality. It is art to live *with* and *through* rather than merely contemplate. My most intimate encounter with Yang's work was in an apartment in Hong Kong where the illumination from a modest assemblage of blinds, lights and wiring welcomed you into a family home. Reflecting back on it, and the glow this work casts, affirms for me Yang's interest in art as a tool, a companion, a toy or a playmate in this game of life.

1 Haegue Yang, 'Influences: Haegue Yang', *Frieze*, no.192, Jan.–Feb. 2018, https://frieze.com/article/influences-haegue-yang, accessed 31 March 2020.
2 The account of Li's life and work in this essay draws on an earlier text: Hammad Nasar, 'Cumbrian Cosmopolitanisms: Li Yuan-chia and Friends', *British Art Studies*, no.12, https://doi.org/10.17658/issn.2058-5462/issue-12/hnasar, accessed 31 March 2020.
3 Guy Brett, 'Space – Life – Time' in *Li Yuan-chia: tell me what is not yet said*, exh. cat., Institute of International Visual Arts, London 2000, p.11.
4 Wall text for the exhibition *View–Point: A Retrospective of Li Yuan-chia* (2014) at the Taipei Fine Art Museum (TFAM). *View–Point* was a collaboration between TFAM and the LYC Foundation, with LYC Foundation Trustees Guy Brett and Nick Sawyer co-curating the exhibition alongside Mei-ching Fang, TFAM's Chief Curator.
5 Li's work was included in *The Other Story: Afro-Asian Artists in Post-war Britain* (1989), curated by Rasheed Araeen at the Hayward Gallery, London, with subsequent touring venues including Wolverhampton Art Gallery, Manchester City Art Gallery and Cornerhouse, Manchester. A posthumous retrospective exhibition, *Li Yuan-chia: tell me what is not yet said* (2001), curated by Guy Brett, was organised by Iniva (Institute of International Visual Arts) at the Camden Arts Centre, London; Abbot Hall Art Gallery and Museum, Kendal; and Palais des Beaux-Arts, Brussels.
6 For instance, Li's work had only a small presence in Tate Britain's *Migrations: Journeys into British Art* (2012); Tate Modern's 2015 display of his work was slightly more expansive, but he was entirely absent from Tate Britain's *Conceptual Art in Britain 1964–1979* (2016).
7 Li had three solo exhibitions and participated in three group shows at the Lisson Gallery between 1967 and 1970.
8 The exhibition *Performing No Thingness* (2016), curated by Nicola Simpson at Norwich University of the Arts, explored the work of Li Yuan-chia, dom sylvester houédard and Ken Cox. The LYC featured prominently in the exhibition *Speech Acts: Reflection-Imagination-Repetition* (24 May 2018–22 April 2019) curated by Hammad Nasar with Kate Jesson at Manchester Art Gallery. The exhibition was accompanied by a symposium, 'The LYC Museum & Art Gallery and the Museum as Practice', 6–7 March 2019. For more details, see https://www.paul-mellon-centre.ac.uk/whats-on/forthcoming/cfp-lyc-museum-and-art-gallery-and-the-museum-as-practice, accessed 31 March 2020.
9 Quoted in Brett 2000, p.10.
10 Yang 2018.
11 Hilary Floe, 'Everything was Getting Smashed: Three Case Studies of Play and Participation', *Tate Papers*, no.22, Autumn 2014. https://www.tate.org.uk/research/publications/tate-papers/22/everything-was-getting-smashed-three-case-studies-of-play-and-participation-1965-71, accessed 8 February 2019.
12 Quoted in Mei-ching Fang, 'More than a Museum: LYC Museum and Art Gallery' in *View–Point: A Retrospective of Li Yuan-chia*, exh. cat., Taipei Fine Art Museum, Taipei 2015, vol.1, p.127.
13 *Space & Freedom* by Helen Petts was commissioned for the exhibition *Speech Acts: Reflection-Imagination-Repetition* at Manchester Art Gallery. It was produced with financial assistance from the Arts Council of England National Lottery Fund and the Li Yuan-chia Foundation, and made use of material from Li's archives at The John Rylands Library, University of Manchester.
14 Extracts from Li Yuan-chia's texts in catalogues (1959), in *View–Point: A Retrospective of Li Yuan-chia*, 2015, vol.3, p.22.

Li Yuan-chia
1+1=1-1 1965
1+1-1 1965

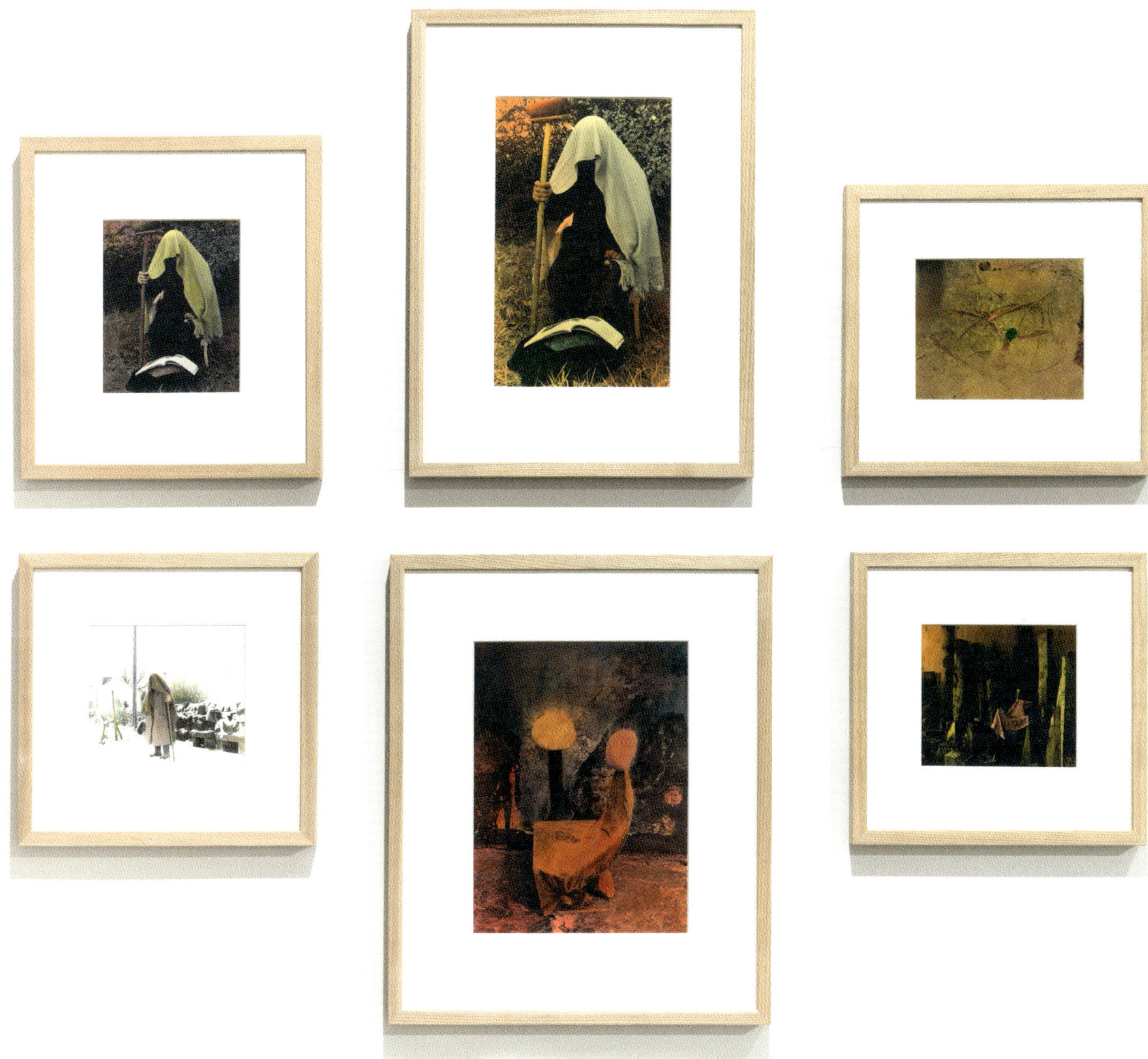

Li Yuan-chia
Untitled 1993

Li Yuan-chia
Untitled 1993–4

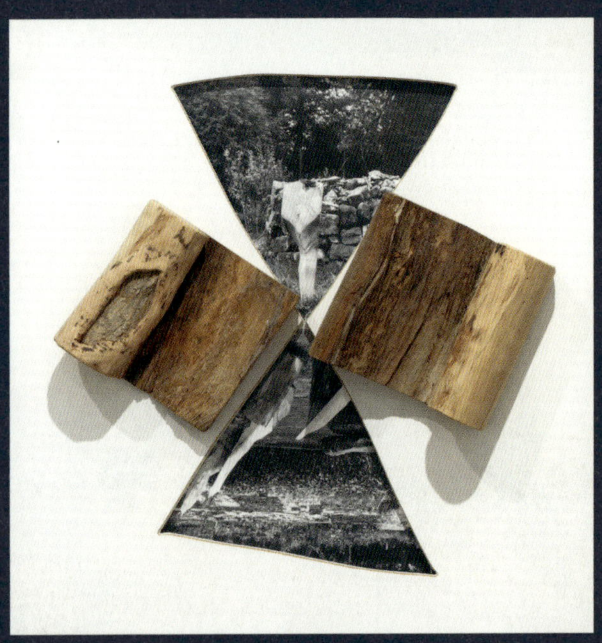

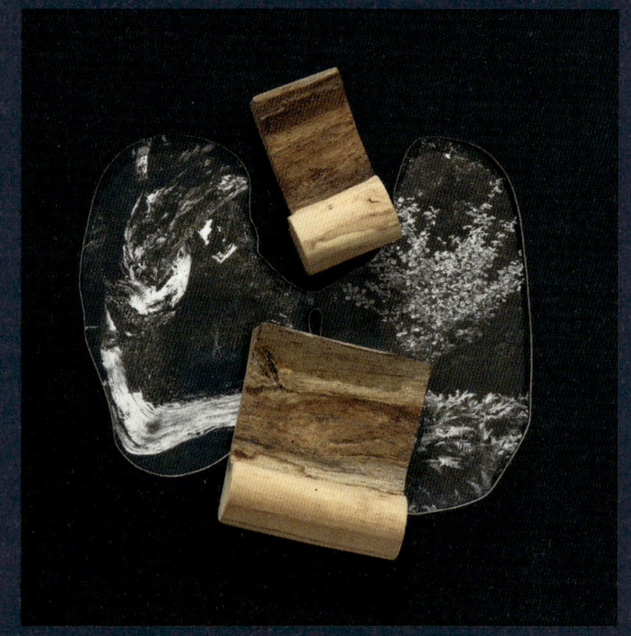

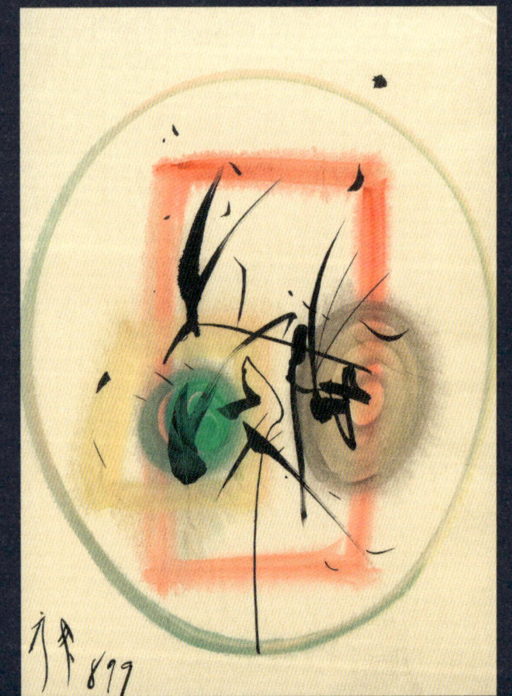

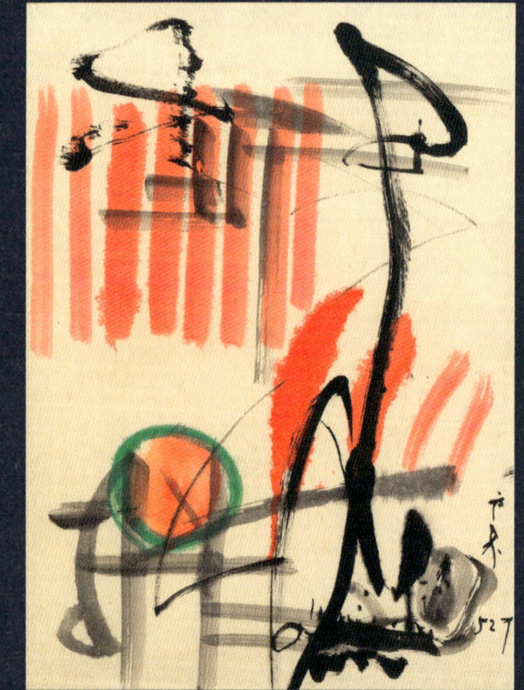

Naum Gabo
Circular Relief c.1925

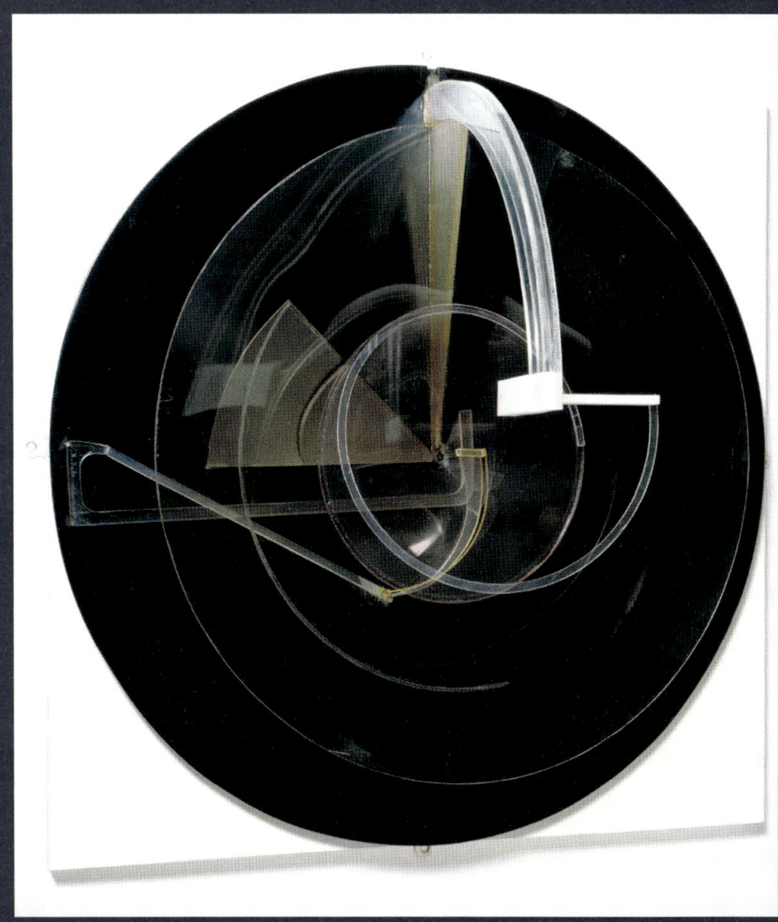

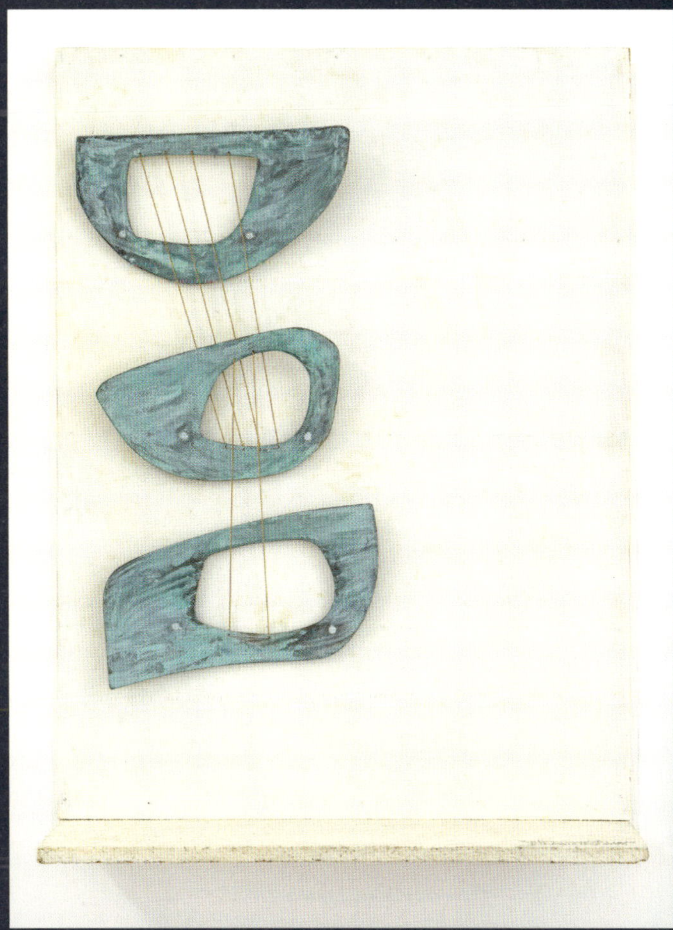

Dame Barbara Hepworth
Maquette, Three Forms in Echelon 1961

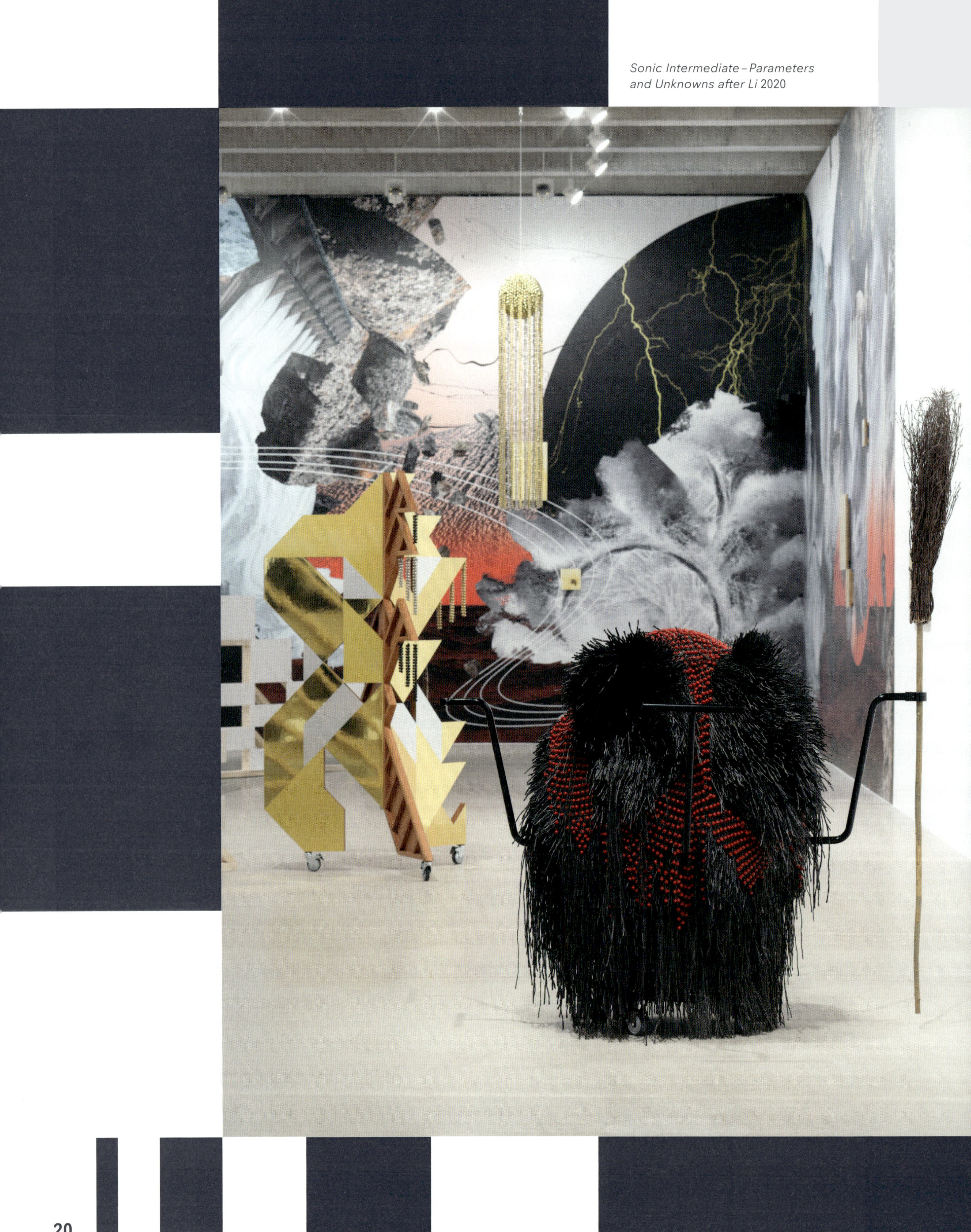

Sonic Intermediate – Parameters and Unknowns after Li 2020

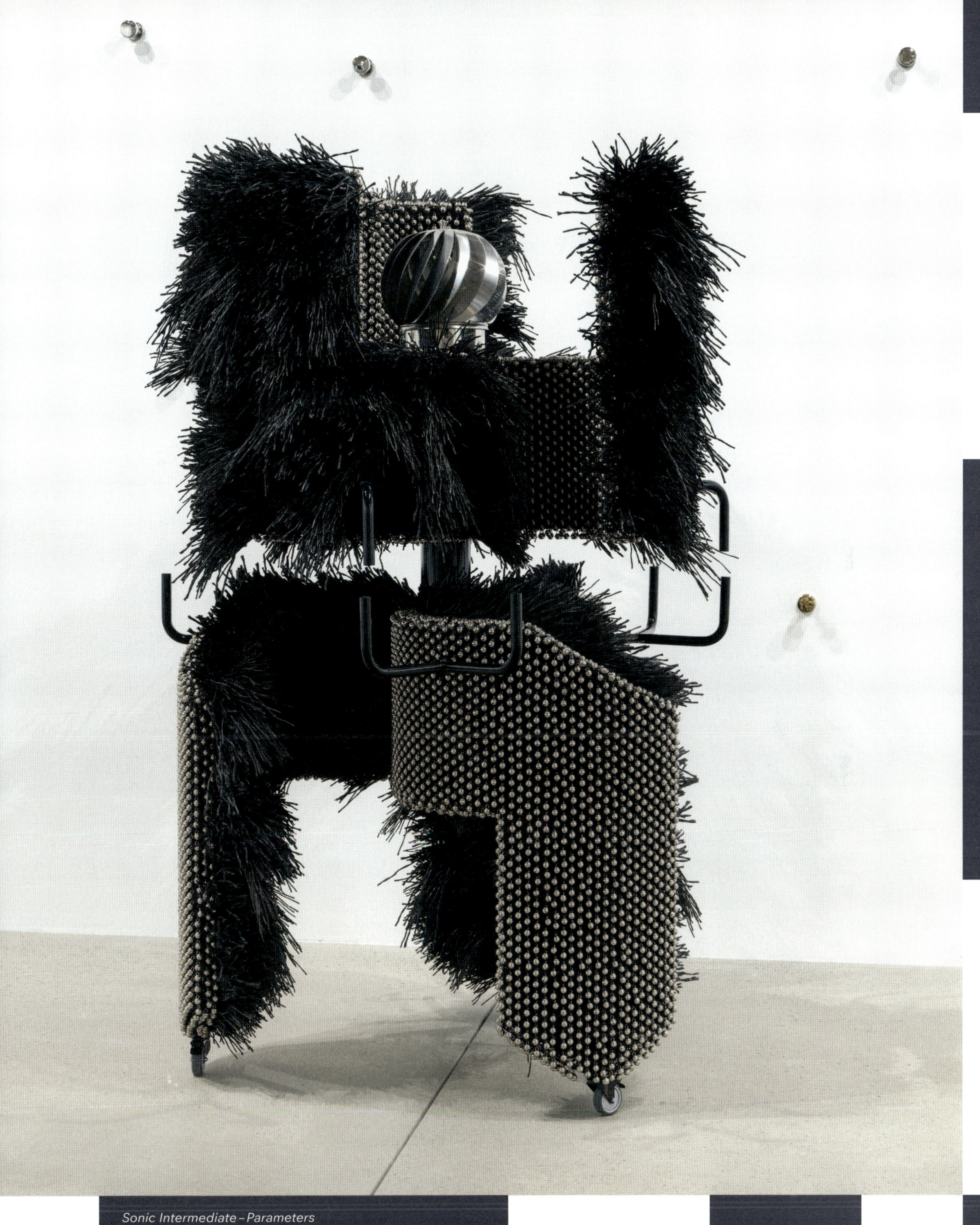

Sonic Intermediate – Parameters and Unknowns after Gabo 2020

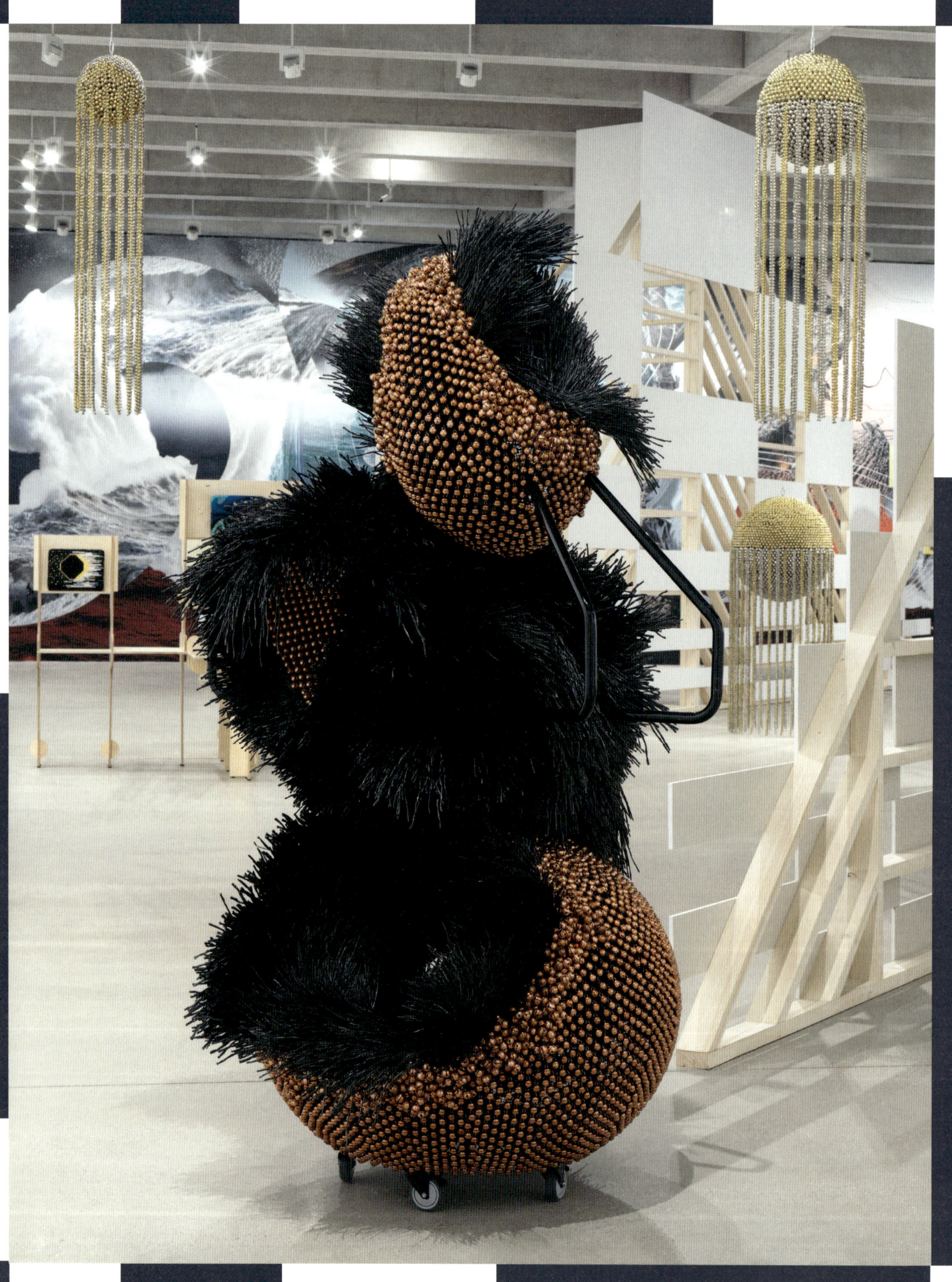

Sonic Intermediate – Parameters and Unknowns after Hepworth 2020

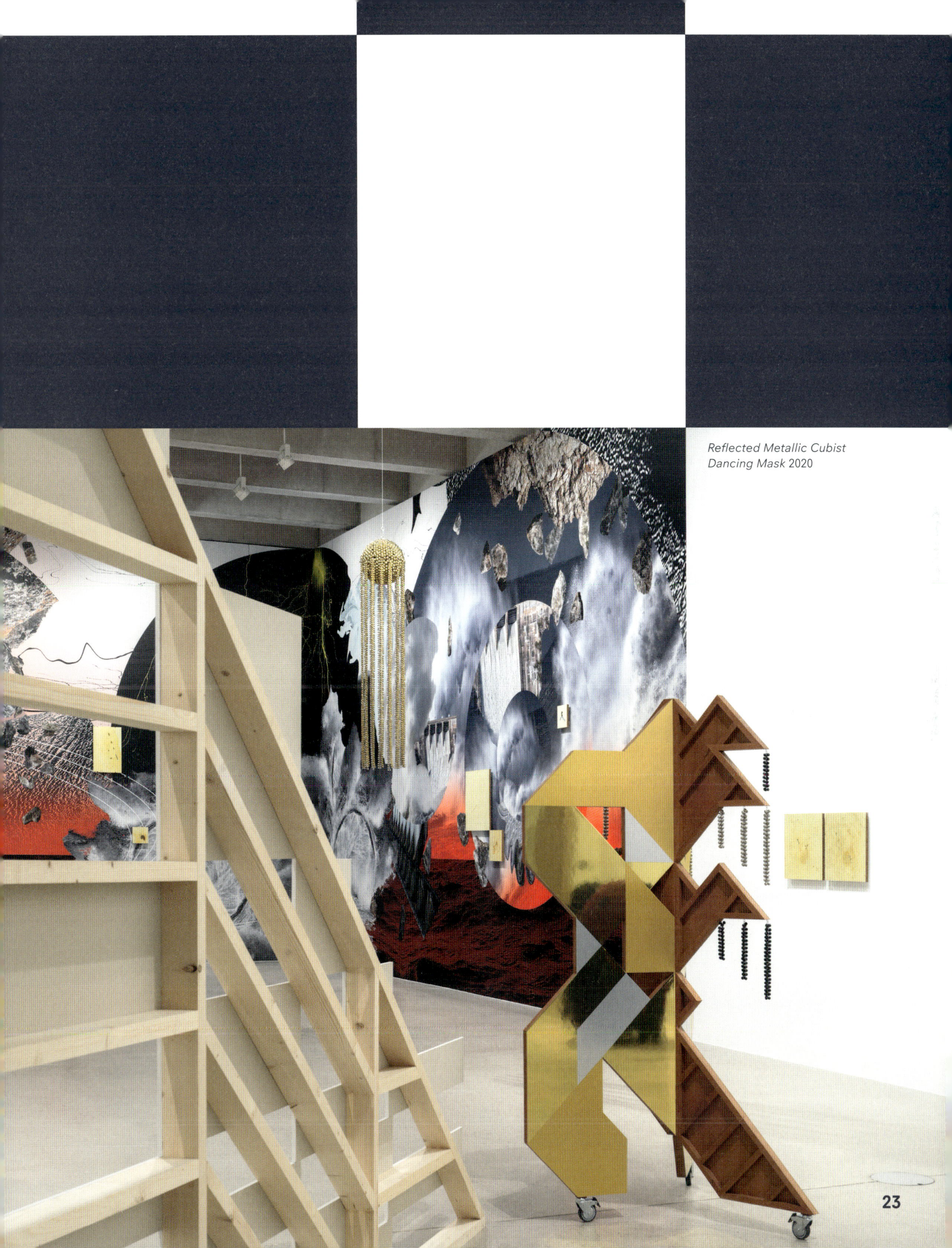

Reflected Metallic Cubist Dancing Mask 2020

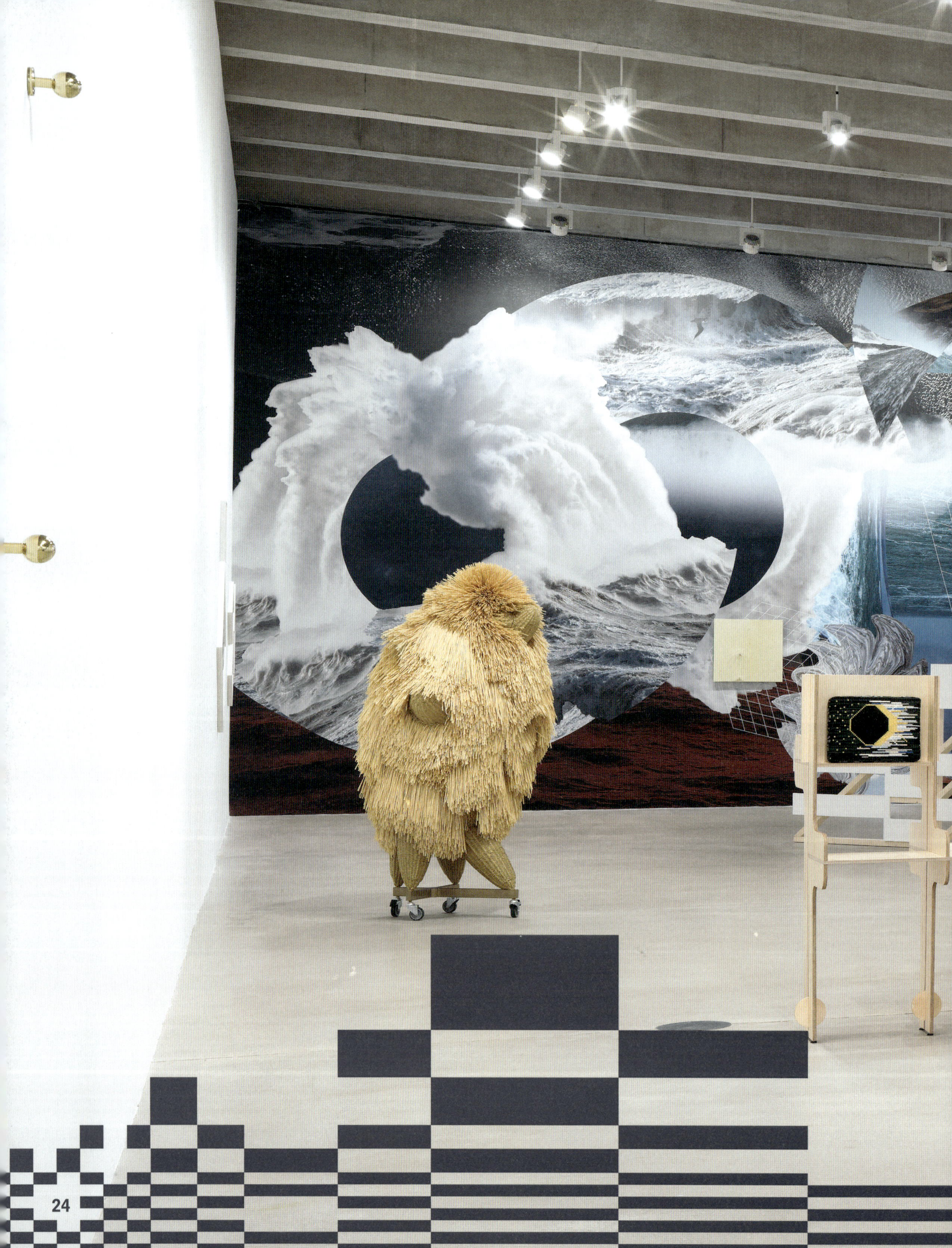

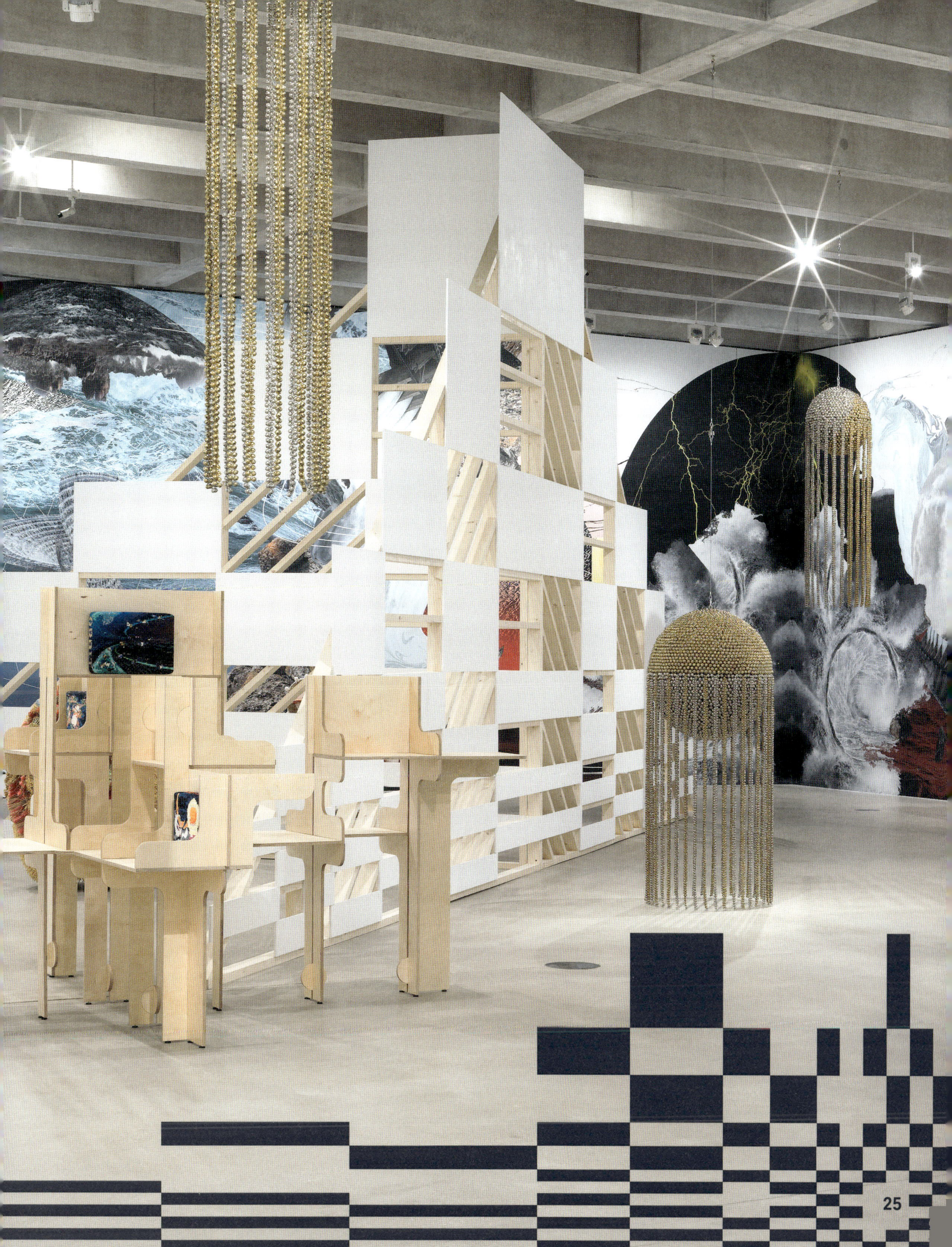

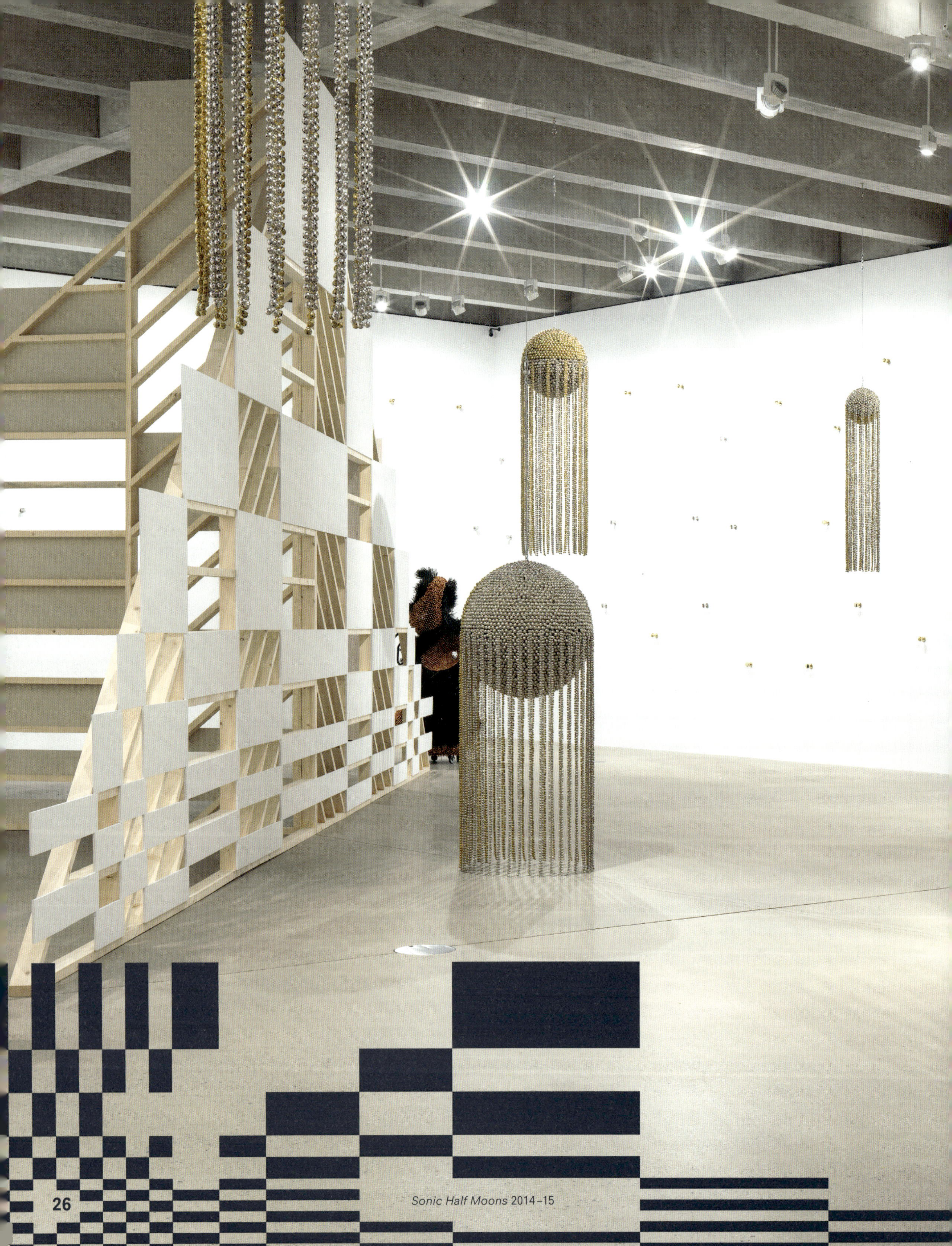

Sonic Half Moons 2014–15

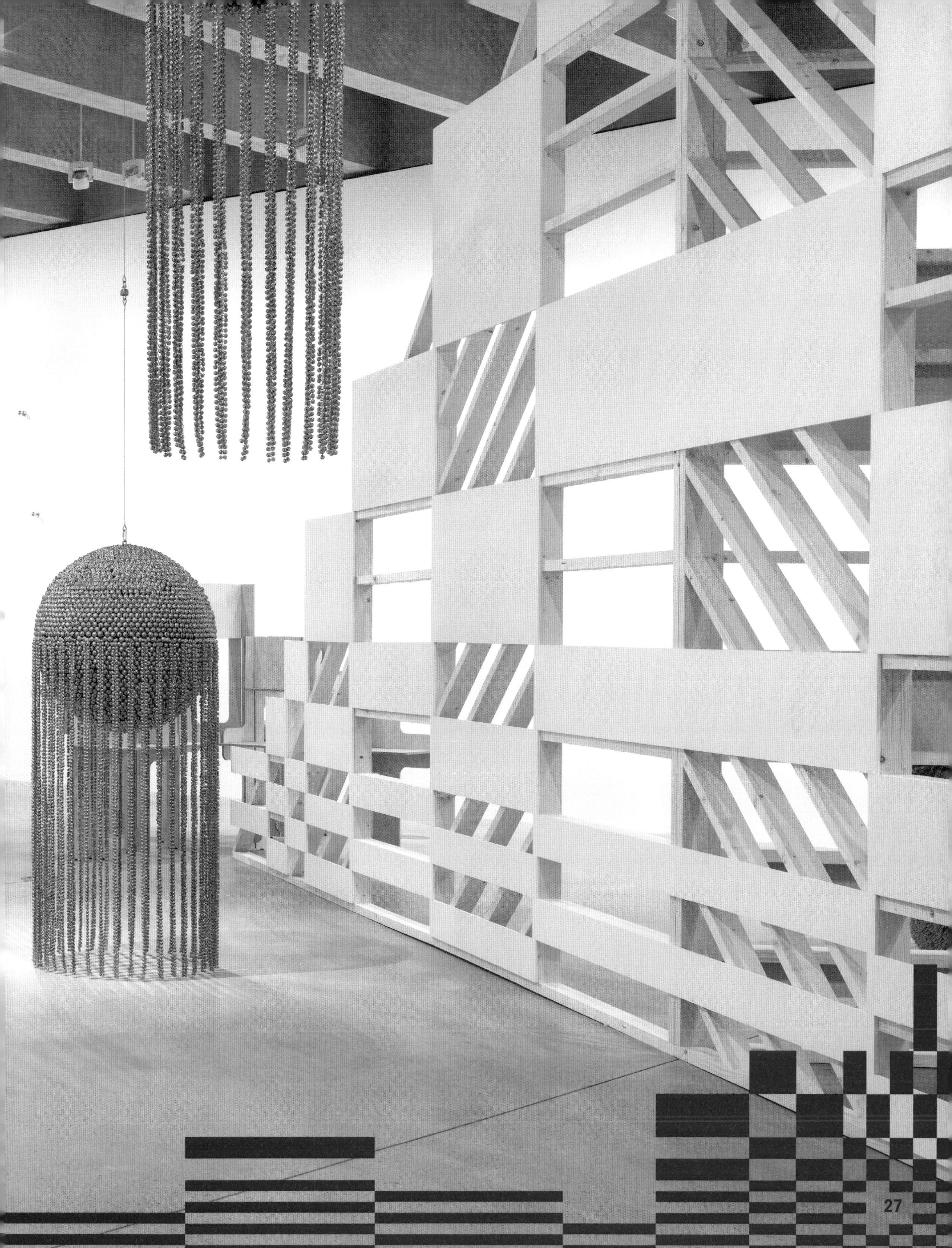

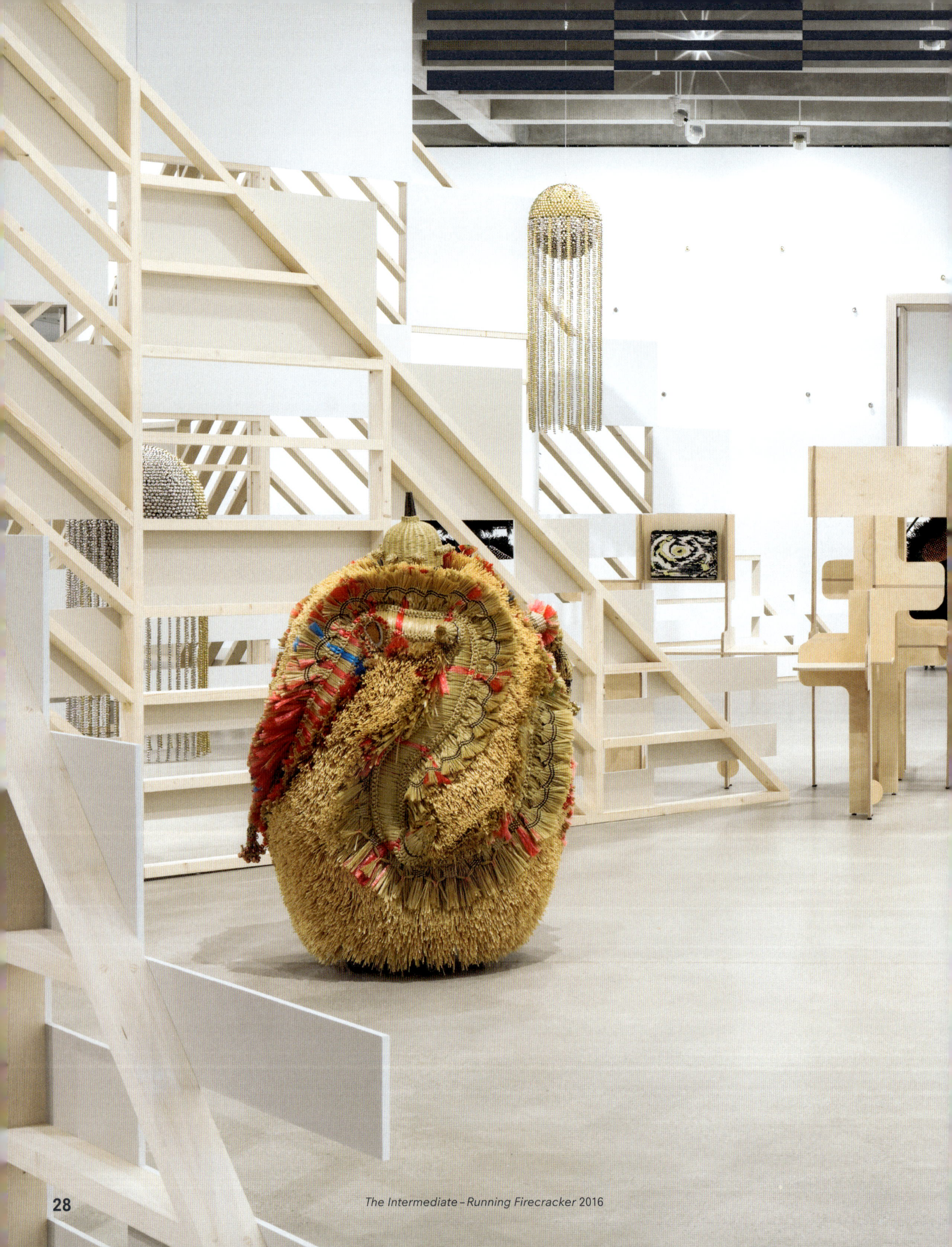

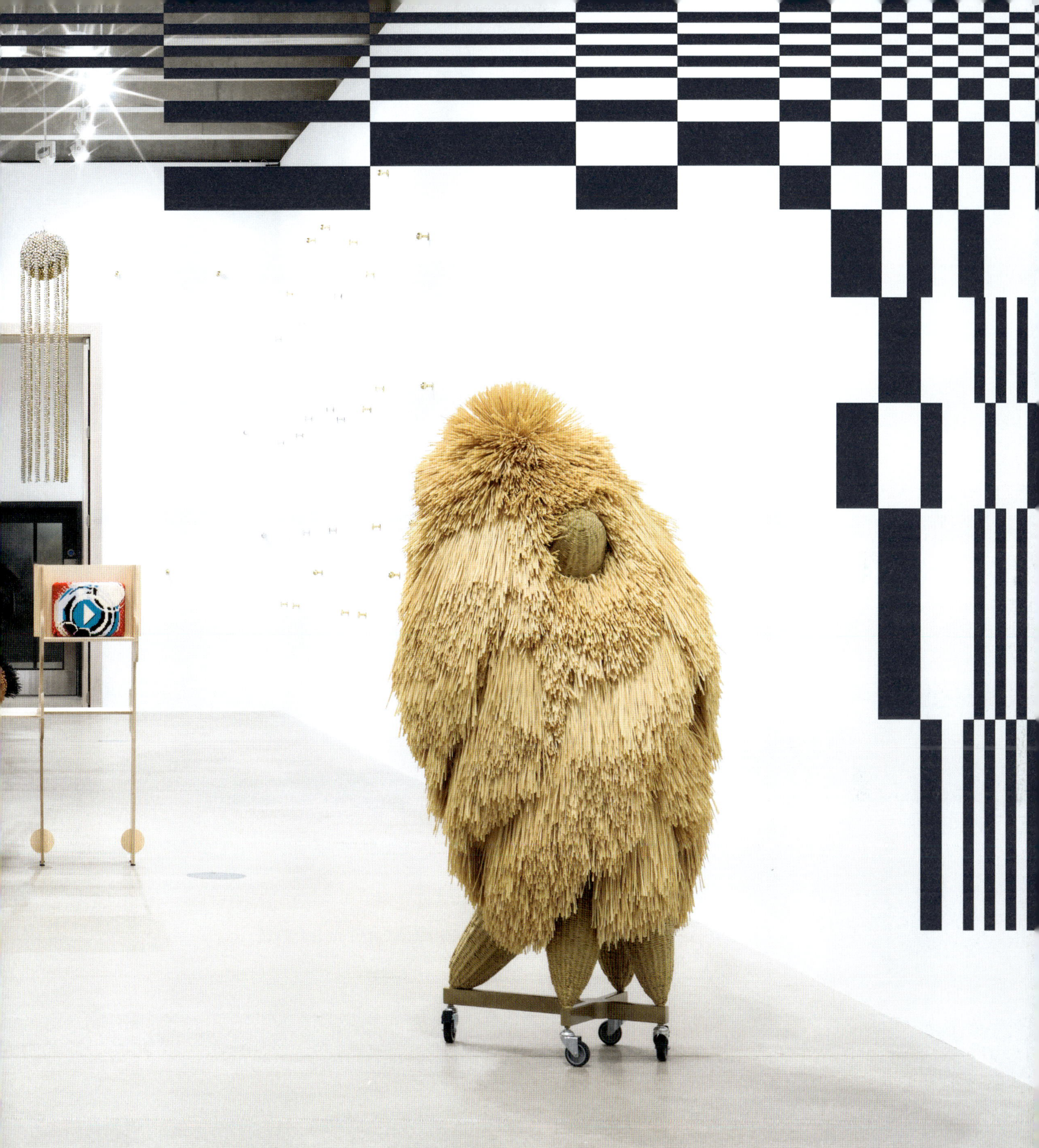

The Intermediate – Tilted Bushy Lumpy Bumpy 2016

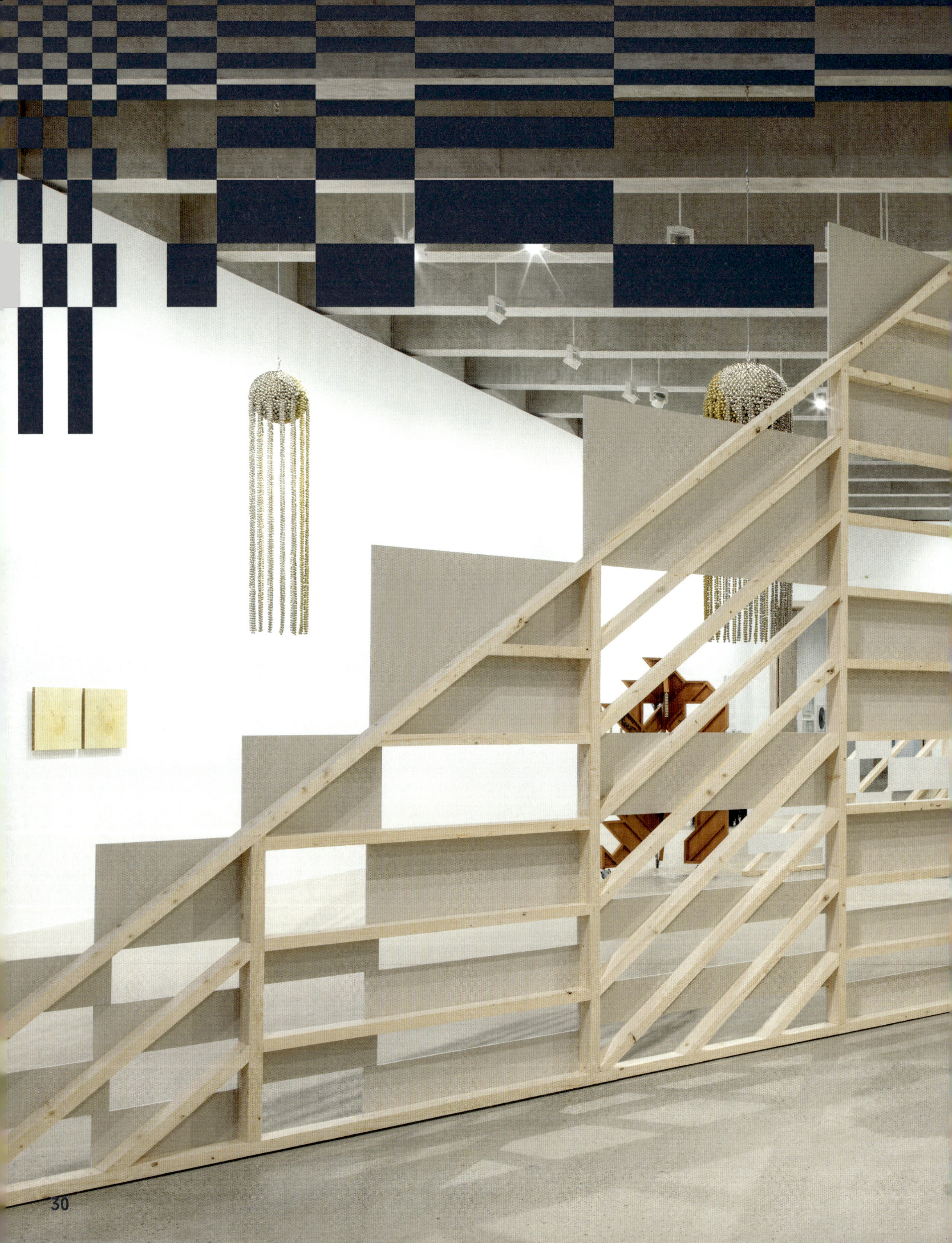

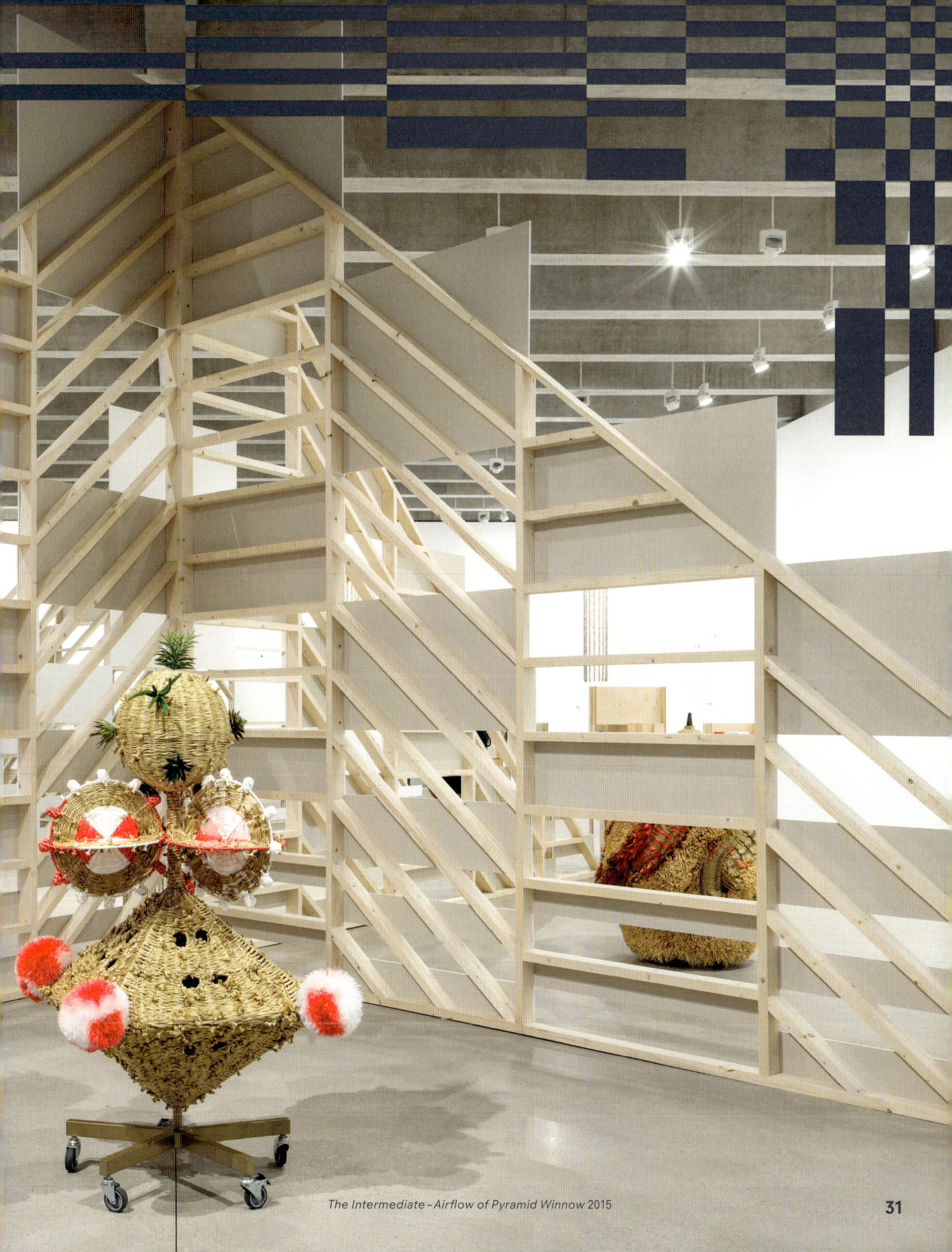

The Intermediate – Airflow of Pyramid Winnow 2015

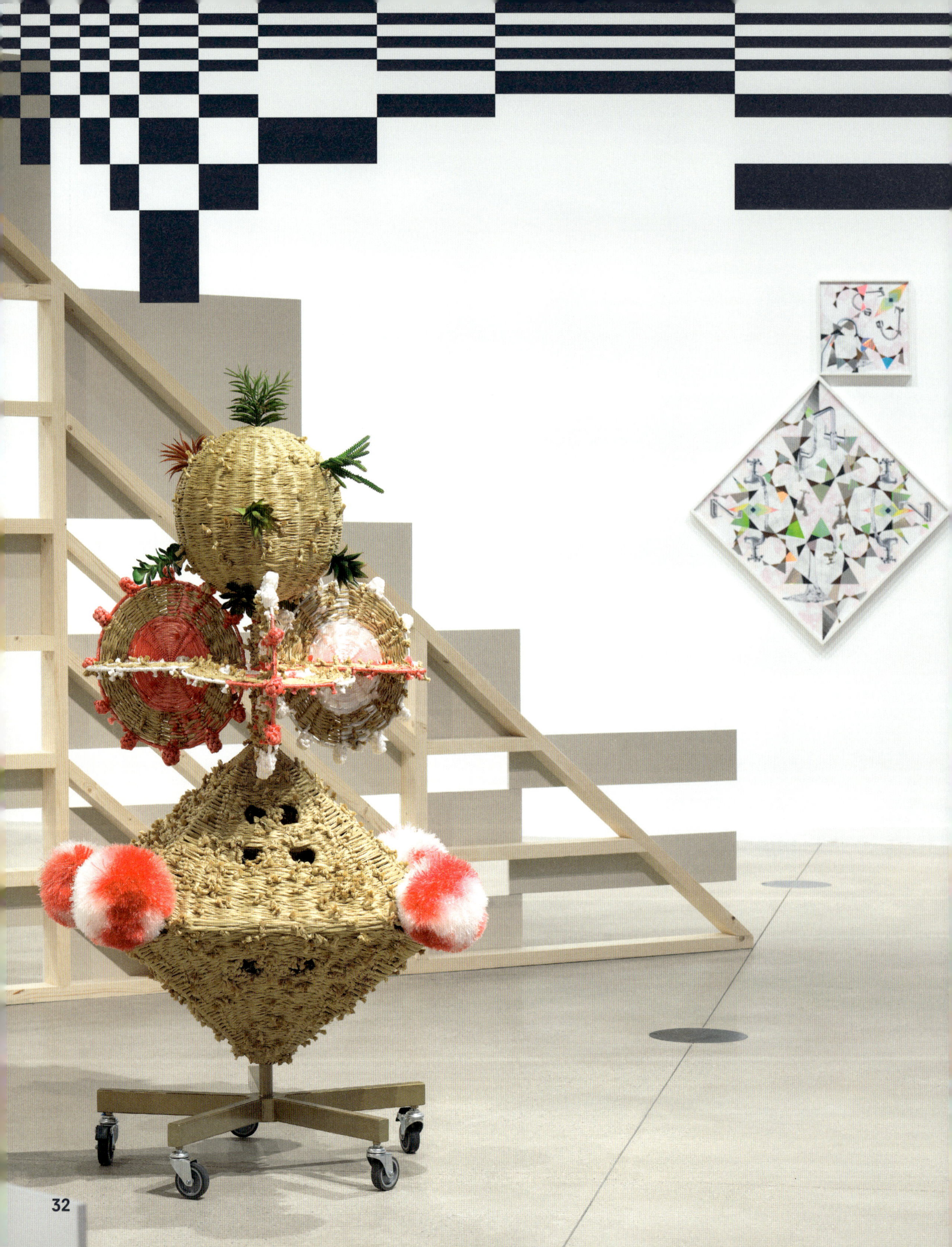

Asymmetrical Encounters

Anne Barlow

Every word Haegue Yang uses in relation to her work is chosen with precision and purpose. The titles of her works and exhibitions are frequently complex or ambiguous, embodying more than one potential meaning or association, and *Strange Attractors* is no exception.

On a scientific level, the term originates in the work of meteorologist and mathematician Edward Lorenz (1917–2008). As part of his research into the degree to which weather could be predicted, Lorenz used mathematics to emulate the non-repeating – or 'non-periodic' – behaviour of natural weather systems, in particular rolling fluid convection (a temperature difference in the atmosphere). To do so, he used a number of differential equations that represented variables such as temperature, pressure and velocity, and processed the data through a computer. What he found was that even the smallest of changes in the initial conditions resulted in highly divergent paths or trajectories, a discovery that was to be highly significant in the study of chaos theory. When plotted graphically this 'strange attractor', or Lorenz attractor, possessed a fractal structure whose movements traced out a shape that resembled a butterfly.[1]

In films, literature and other media, the 'butterfly effect' has come to refer to those instances within a narrative where a seemingly insignificant event has an unexpected and often dramatic outcome in the future.[2] As an exhibition title, *Strange Attractors* speaks to our prevailing desire to predict outcomes with certainty, in a world that continues to be shaped by chaotic natural forces as well as by the ongoing impact of human existence on our environment.

The phrase also suggests myriad potential associations within the exhibition itself – not only across different bodies of Yang's own work, but also between her work and that of the other artists she has chosen to include: Li Yuan-chia (1929–94), Barbara Hepworth (1903–75) and Naum Gabo (1890–1977).

The configuration of the show sets the conditions for such 'encounters'. Yang's own work fills the main space in Tate St Ives's new extension with an extraordinary installation of architectural interventions, sculptures and wallpaper, while the curved, sea-facing gallery hosts the delicate and almost ethereal sculptures *Non-Indépliables, nues* 2010/2020. Between these two, a smaller connecting gallery presents a selection of work by Li Yuan-chia, alongside sculptures by Hepworth and Gabo. This transitional space becomes a kind of 'lens' through which to experience not only Yang's expansive practice, but also the work and legacy of Li, Hepworth and Gabo, in fresh ways. Visual, sensorial and even spiritual connections and resonances can be felt through this asymmetrical and imaginary encounter across time and place.

The Sonic Intermediates

Yang articulates the main gallery through dramatic free-standing wall structures, with perforations inspired by a traditional geometric Philippine Binakul 'whirlwind' textile pattern.[3] Alluding to the wind and the waves, this abstract design creates the representation of a sphere within a two-dimensional design through 'positive and negative' coloured threads. As a pattern, it is believed to offer protection against malevolent spirits by confusing them through the optical illusion of volume and movement.

Opening up sightlines across the room, these permeable wall structures create a diagonal passageway across the centre in which *Sonic Half Moons* 2014–15 encased with patterns of nickel and brass plated bells are suspended. The gallery is also populated by existing and new sculptures from Yang's *Intermediates* series, and other works specially created for the exhibition including *Non-Linear and Non-Periodic Dynamics* 2020, a panoramic wallpaper piece. In combination, these create an otherworldly landscape in which uncanny and seemingly disparate ideas, cultures and time periods coexist.

As a body of work, *The Intermediates* 2015–ongoing incorporates elements such as synthetic straw, twine and artificial plants, powder-coated steel mesh, frames or stands, bells and castors. These anthropomorphic 'creatures' seem at once both ancient and futuristic. Works such as *The Intermediate – Airflow of Pyramid Winnow* 2015, *The Intermediate – Running Firecracker* 2016 and *The Intermediate – Tilted Bushy Lumpy Bumpy* 2016 are formally unique in terms of their shapes and elements, but they nonetheless remain connected. As Chus Martínez writes, 'Every sculpture is different and yet clearly belongs to the same "species"'.[4]

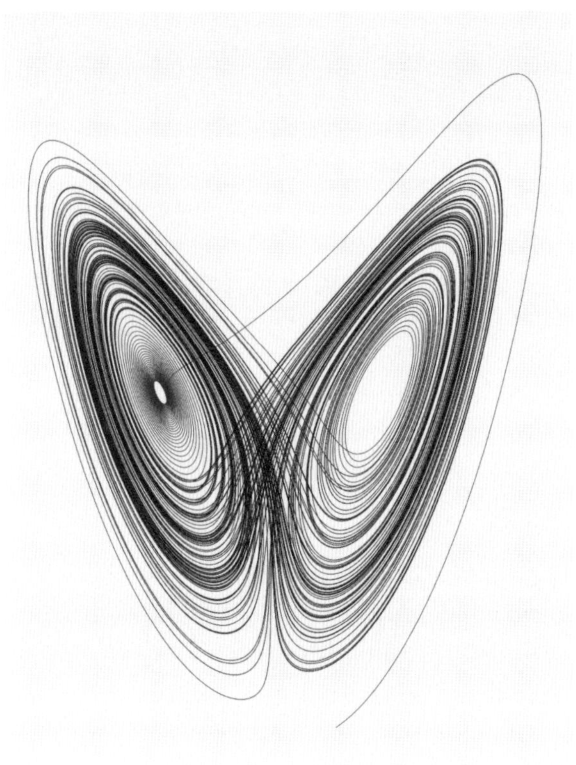

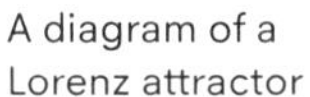
A diagram of a Lorenz attractor

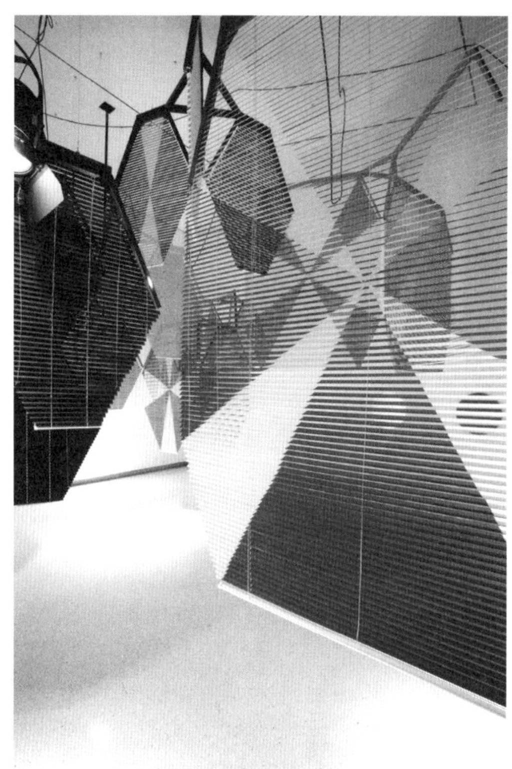

Haegue Yang, *Three Kinds* 2008. Installation view of *Life on Mars*, the 55th Carnegie International, Carnegie Museum of Art, Pittsburgh, USA, 2008

For this exhibition, Yang has created a new sculptural ensemble, *Sonic Intermediates – Three Differential Equations* 2020, that comprises individual works with the title of *Parameters and Unknowns after Li*, *Hepworth* and *Gabo* respectively. While referring to these pioneering figures, the overarching title of the group also harks back to Lorenz's use of three differential equations to analyse atmospheric convection. Here, 'parameters' and 'unknowns' refer to terms that are 'known' and 'unknown' within these equations, which in themselves are non-linear. Such references act as a metaphor for the real and imagined aspects of each *Intermediate*, and the possible resonances among and across the three.

Hepworth and Gabo were part of an artistic circle in London in the 1930s and each separately moved to Cornwall with the outbreak of the Second World War in 1939.[5] As Hammad Nasar observes in his essay, Hepworth and Gabo were also part of Li Yuan-chia's exhibition programme at the LYC Museum and Art Gallery in Cumbria, so in a sense there were moments when the three artists occupied the same 'orbits' even if they were not physically in the same place at the same time.

Parameters and Unknowns after Li sits low to the ground. Four side bars extend outwards like arms, with tufts of black artificial straw protruding through holes in the mesh of red brass plated bells lain over its body. It grasps a broom, much as a seated Li, his head covered in a blanket, appears in the similarly 'faceless' self-portrait *Untitled* 1993, from Li's series of hand-tinted photographs taken in the grounds of the LYC Museum. The mesh that emulates the blanket is red, a colour that for Li symbolised blood, or life.[6]

Yang's interest in Li's work is explored in depth in this publication by Hammad Nasar, who puts forward several possible areas of connection between the artists. These include approaches that invite participation, the use of fine art and craft practices, and a way of working that both conceals and reveals, giving both artists' work a quality of 'translucence'.[7]

Yang's research visit to Cumbria in September 2019 was also crucial to the exhibition's development. Visiting the former LYC Museum, Yang learned more about Li's life and work through those who had known him or who were studying the impact and legacy of his work within larger art histories. The writer Diana Yeh has posited that Li's practice demonstrates 'the necessity of reconfiguring modern art histories to include complex translocal crossings and alternative modernisms that continue to be obscured by Eurocentric and nation-state discourses'.[8] Here, there seems to be an affinity with the way in which Yang's own work, which incorporates elements and references from multiple cultures and art histories, also makes one-dimensional readings impossible.

The cooler, black and silver tones of *Parameters and Unknowns after Gabo* evoke Gabo's *Circular Relief* c.1925, while its material components are quite distinct. Radiating out from a central vertical core, the external planes of the lower section are covered in nickel plated bells, with black straw on the inner face, an order which is reversed in the upper part. Much of the sculpture's interior and exterior can be viewed simultaneously, even more so when it is activated through the handles on its sides, which sets the upper and lower sections moving anti-clockwise and clockwise respectively. Planar and metallic, but in a different way to Gabo's own early sculptures, its 'head' is represented by a turbine vent that can be manually rotated.

Parameters and Unknowns after Hepworth reflects Hepworth's interest in natural forms and her use of the hole, or void, in sculptures such as *Oval Sculpture (No. 2)* 1943 and *Spring* 1966. Unlike Hepworth's often pristine creations, this is however an altogether 'wilder' form, with black artificial straw sprouting from curved forms covered in copper plated bells. The frequent use of tripartite forms in Hepworth's work, such as *Three Forms* 1935, *Three Forms Vertical (Offering)* 1967 and *Maquette, Three Forms in Echelon* 1961 (displayed in this exhibition), is repeated in the interconnected forms of Yang's *Intermediate*.[9]

Considered as a grouping, there is also an echo here of Yang's earlier work *Three Kinds* 2008. Though the historical context that inspired it is quite different, the earlier work similarly explored the 'learning' and 'unlearning' of the narratives around three historical figures and their triangular relationship.[10]

The pagan and folkloric

For Yang, the word *Intermediate* 'refers to medium, in shamanic terms, or the mediation between different dimensions. In my sculptures, it's about taking something ancient and bringing it to the present'.[11]

The Intermediates are hybrid forms, drawing on folk traditions from a wide range of historic and contemporary sources, as well as on Yang's ongoing research into rituals across multiple cultures – from shamanic practices in Korea to Hindu traditions to pagan practices throughout Europe. Yang often adapts materials and processes associated with weaving, knotting, crocheting and knitting to create elements of her sculptures. The resulting forms reference the 'hand-made' aspects of these practices, but at the same time appear futuristic or supernatural through her use of artificial rather than natural elements, such as plastic raffia string and artificial straw.

Yang's working approach breaks down traditional hierarchies between fine art and craft, much as artist Sophie Taeuber-Arp (1889–1943), whose work remains an important touchstone for Yang, worked fluidly across fine and applied art, figuration and abstraction. Situated within an art historical context, Yang's quasi-pagan work similarly counters the 'supposed opposition of pre-modern and modern aesthetics, traditional craftsmanship and the Western canon of abstraction'.[12]

Bells, which Yang uses in *Sonic Intermediates* as well as in other series such as *Sonic Figures*, *Dress Vehicles* and *Sonic Half Moons*, are objects that have been used in religious ceremonies or acts of ritual for centuries. As such, in Yang's work they carry associations with both sound and movement, so that each sculpture they adorn possesses a kind of 'internal' sound that becomes audible when activated through human intervention.

The *Sonic Half Moons* create patterns of light and sound, 'dissolving' and then solidifying again as their physical movement subsides, while their spheric forms communicate inherent movement, even when still. As the curator and writer Doryun Chong has pointed out, the idea of rotation in Yang's work metaphorically 'suggests cycle and recurrence – such as seasons, life and death … To be more precise, in planetary terms, rotation is existence per se (life on Earth and the Earth itself would come to an end if it stopped spinning)'.[13]

Strange Attractors builds on Yang's ongoing research into the pagan and folkloric in its references to the local context of Cornwall. A new work, *Mundus Cushion – Yielding X* 2020, draws inspiration from the church pews and kneeler cushions in St Senara's Church in Zennor, West Penwith. Yang has abstracted both the design of the benches and the kneelers (which traditionally depict animals, landscapes, and religious and domestic symbols) into her own unique explorations of the sacred and the secular. As a group, the cushions – *Nimbus*, *Orbit*, *Twilight*, *Launch*, *Eclipse*, *Climate*, *Sphere* and *Tempest* – evoke associations with astronomy, meteorology and cosmology. Some hark back to the motifs and aesthetics of the original cushions, such as the evocative *Eclipse*, while others clearly reference the contemporary, as seen in Yang's use of the triangular 'play' symbol associated with media files in *Launch*.

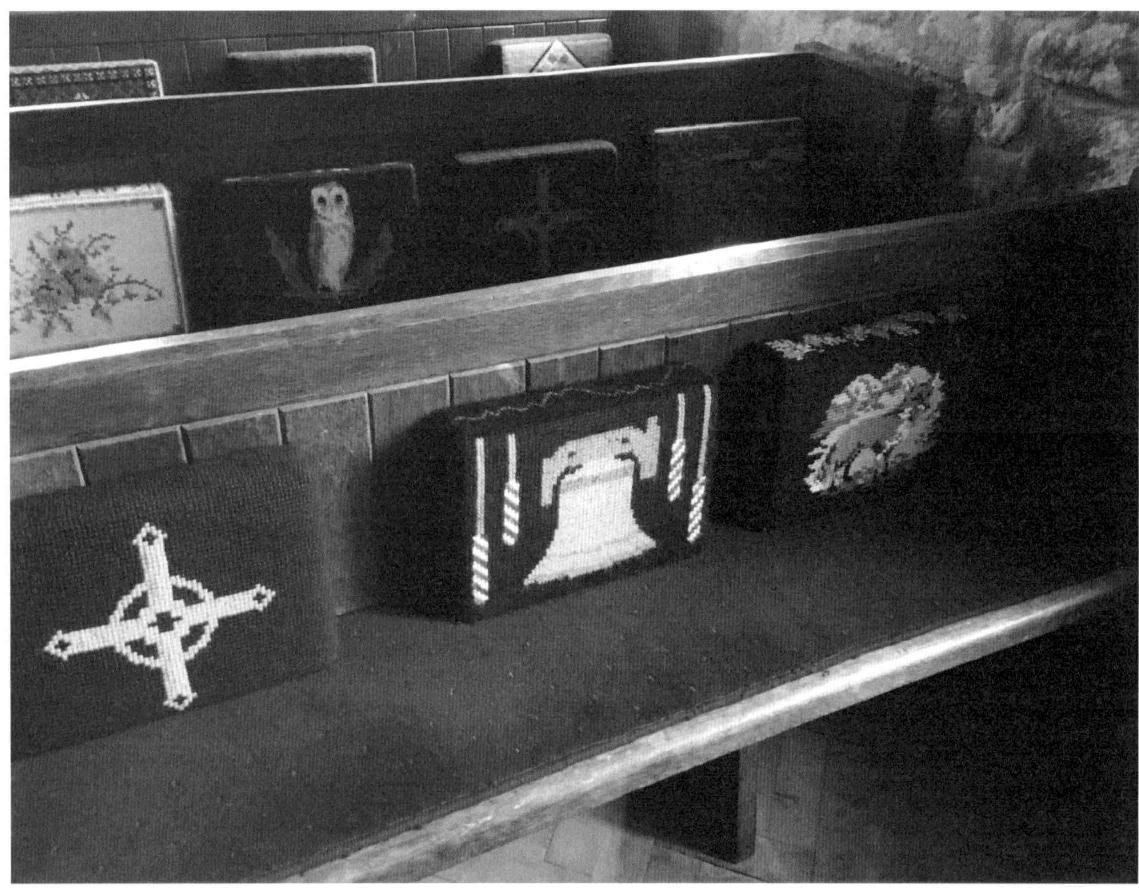

Kneeler cushions within St Senara's Church in Zennor, West Penwith, Cornwall

Yang also draws on associations with Cornwall in two *Trustworthies* created for the exhibition. The first *Trustworthies* were made in 2010 and are typically created with materials such as graph paper, security patterns on the insides of envelopes, laser prints, origami paper and self-adhesive holographic vinyl film. At Tate St Ives, both of the new *Trustworthies*, along with Yang's expansive wallpaper piece, make references to water: *Fluidity on Nonagonal Crystal Matrix – Trustworthy #400* 2020 includes images of water taps, while *Cornish Healing Catch – Trustworthy #403* 2020 features mops, buckets, stones, fishing cages and trap floats, within complex geometric compositions.

Handles

Geometrical shapes feature elsewhere in the main gallery in the form of eleven nonagons, marked out by handles, which span the walls of the entrance and exit of the gallery.[14] The handles chart out the nine points of the Enneagram, an ancient symbol reintroduced to the modern world by G.I. Gurdjieff (1866–1949), the renowned Russian spiritualist. Gurdjieff considered the nonagonal pattern 'the fundamental hieroglyph of a universal language', a dynamic symbol on which different systems of knowledge could be mapped.[15]

A key strand of Gurdjieff's teachings was to combine body, emotions and intellect in a way that facilitated the development of a 'whole' and balanced person. He created Movements, or 'Sacred Dances', choreographies of precise and mostly asymmetrical gestures that were not necessarily meant to be publicly staged but rather performed by his students. Yang's interest in Gurdjieff lies in this 'expanded notion of movement'[16] and in how movement can evoke other sensorial effects. 'Movement is an interesting word because it brings all different dimensions: physical, emotional, sociopolitical. And if I can approach movement without reducing these dimensions, I would consider my attempt successful.'[17]

As with many of the visual vocabularies Yang develops around standardised products or household items, she considers the handle in both a functional and metaphorical way. As objects utilised in a physical action to open or close, or turn something on or off, in Yang's work they are 'intermediary' objects between different spaces or states. Handles become symbols of 'beings who are between borders or distinct belongingness' – an attribute they appear to share with *The Intermediates*.[18]

The presence of the *Sonic Intermediates* in the same space-time also brings to mind Yang's use of the term

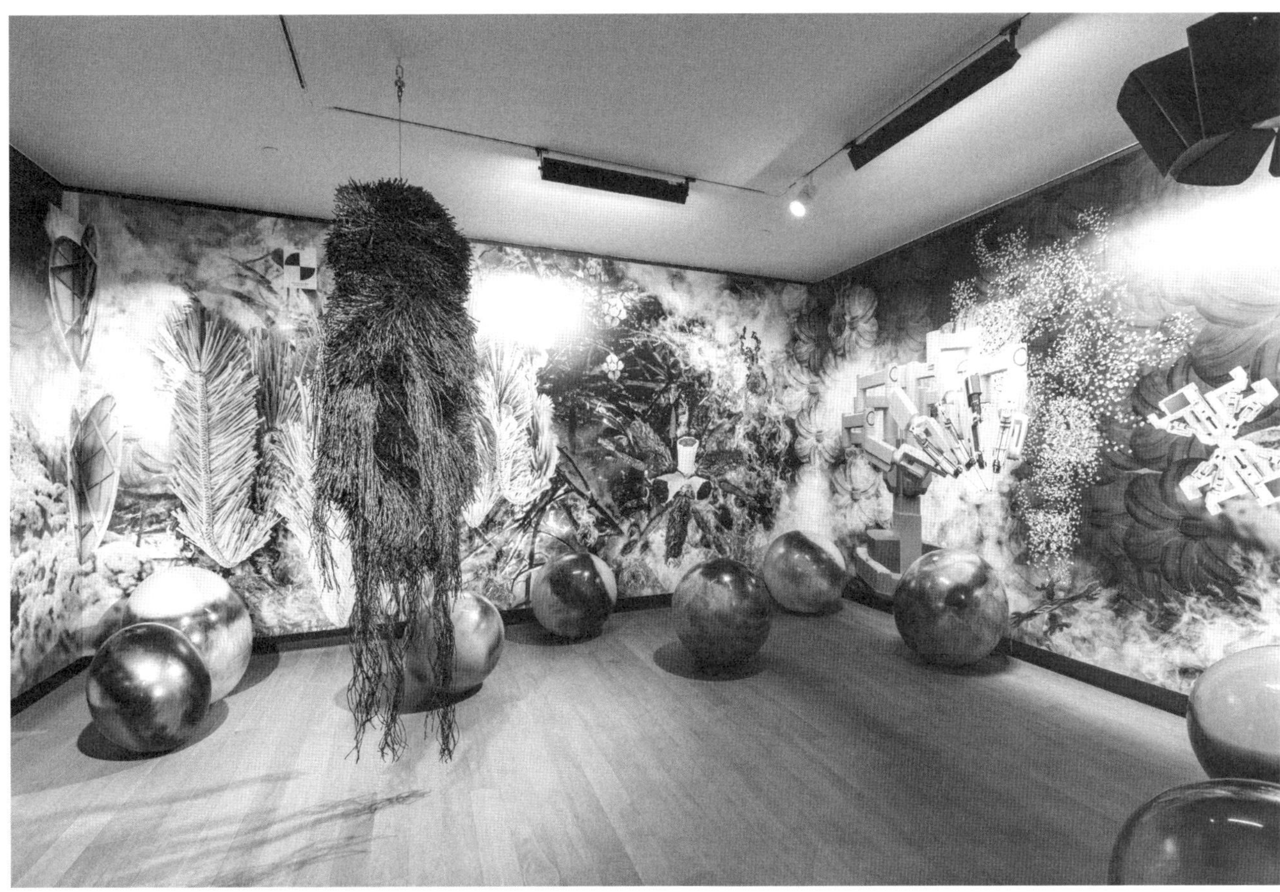

Haegue Yang, *Incubation and Exhaustion – Version Istanbul* 2019. Installation view of *The Seventh Continent*, 16th Istanbul Biennial, Turkey, 2019

'condensation' – a natural phenomenon when different temperatures coexist on a surface where droplets might emerge – to relate to different worlds or conditions that are able to maintain their own 'temperatures' or identities without compromise. Interestingly, in considering the relationship of the three *Sonic Intermediates*, we recall Gurdjieff's postulate that only when three independent forces come together can things change – a dynamism created through asymmetry.

Compression

Strands of thinking, or preoccupations, span and evolve across Yang's recent installations. Her interest in systems and processes around the prediction of weather and climate patterns was particularly evident in two recent wallpaper installations. Made in collaboration with Studio Manuel Raeder and exhibited at the 16th Istanbul Biennial *The Seventh Continent*[19] – a term that refers to a huge mass of waste in the oceans – Yang's wallpaper work *Incubation and Exhaustion – Version Istanbul* 2019 shows secchi disks, which measure turbidity, or the relative clarity or transparency of water. These reference polluted seas, while the inclusion of chillies suggests the ever-increasing rate of global warming.

Similarly, the title of Yang's recent show at The Bass in Miami, *In the Cone of Uncertainty*, refers to the probable track of the centre of a storm, which is particularly apt for Miami's precarious geographic location, where hurricanes and cyclones are common.[20] Informed by Yang's research into the climate and demographics of Miami Beach, the site-specific wallpaper piece *Coordinates of Speculative Solidarity* 2019 depicts abstracted meteorological diagrams and graphics, aerial views of homes, landscapes and communities that are often bound together in the face of adversity.

This compression of geographic, temporal and meteorological references into a flat surface is continued in Yang's new wallpaper work created for the Tate St Ives exhibition. *Non-Linear and Non-Periodic Dynamics* crosses two walls in the gallery and obliquely references the topography, coastlines and ancient sites of the West Penwith landscape that Yang toured on a research visit to Cornwall in 2018. Panoramic vistas depict wild weather and seas, with imagery that is somewhat ominous in parts. In its collapsed and concealed images, the wallpaper work suggests the presence of hidden layers with the potential to be released into three dimensions.

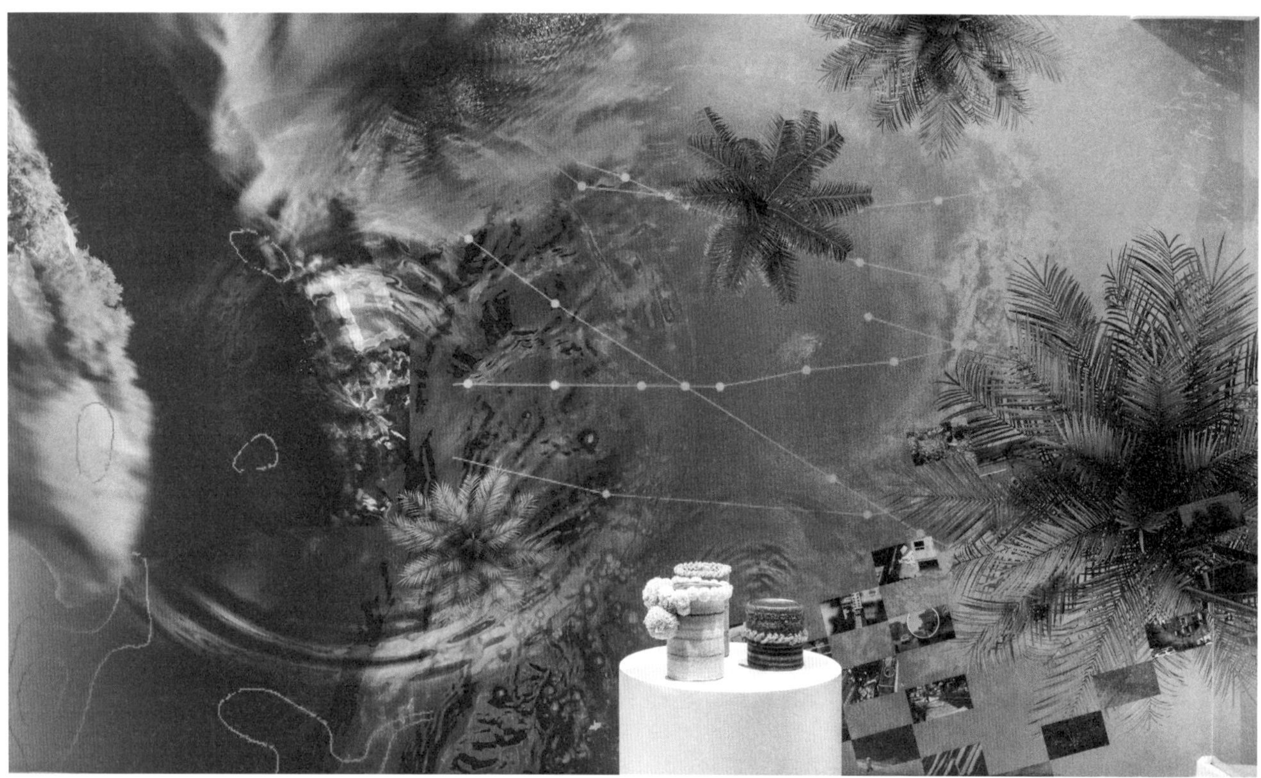

Haegue Yang, *Coordinates of Speculative Solidarity* 2019. Installation view of *In the Cone of Uncertainty*, The Bass, Miami Beach, USA, 2019

Installed over the wallpaper are small-scale *Lacquer Paintings* (ongoing since 1994) that reference the traditions of lacquerware in Asia. Made of chipboard covered in wood varnish, and in several cases incorporating other objects, their surfaces contain elements such as dust, hair, insects, and seeds, captured over time in the drying surface of the varnish. In contrast to the typically smooth finish of lacquered objects, these works are like 'microclimates' that incorporate the influence of their immediate environments during the process of their making. These have evocative titles such as *Crimped Shooting Star* 2019, represented by a metal spring, *Pin-eyed Dead Leaf Butterfly* 2019, with antennae made of two round-headed pins, and *Parachuted Softly* 2019, which conveys allusions to air and movement through the snipped tops of mesh produce bags.

Folding, unfolding and non-folding

Ideas around the concepts of 'folding', 'unfolding' and 'non-folding' are brought together in two bodies of work in the sea-facing gallery: the works on paper *Non-Folding – Geometric Tipping* 2015[21] and the sculptures *Non-Indépliables, nues*.

Across her work, Yang has used industrial and domestic objects such as venetian blinds, turbine vents, air conditioners and tin cans. In *Non-Indépliables, nues*, she appropriates the familiar domestic object of the drying rack, designed to host the wet clothing of other bodies. Yang first used a drying rack in 2006 in her seminal project *Sadong 30*, for which she installed works in her late grandmother's house, and as an object it has since appeared in a variety of forms.[22]

In *Non-Indépliables, nues*, the racks are covered with cords, strings and light bulbs which prevent them from carrying out their original function. These are naked, skeletal structures, with an anthropomorphic quality that here is perhaps less about them taking the shape of a 'creature' – as in *The Intermediates* – and more in how they themselves relate to 'the human body and its operation'.[23] As Yang has reflected: 'For me it is curiously exciting when something appears alien but simultaneously demonstrates an affinity to the human realm.'[24]

The pairing of *Non-Indépliables, nues* and *Non-Folding – Geometric Tipping* is a poignant one. In origami, the act of folding transforms flat paper into a three-dimensional object that occupies and 'holds' space. *Non-Folding – Geometric Tipping* was created through a process of laying origami models onto paper, turning them and spray-painting them so that each subsequent repositioning is captured in outline. The tones and 'shadows' created across the paper represent an important concept in Yang's work: that of 'non-folding', which banishes the 'original, positive shapes to the realm of the undetectable, as if the originals never existed in the first place'.[25] Drying racks share that potential to be both two and three-dimensional, but unlike origami, where a flat piece of paper is transformed through the act of folding into three-dimensional forms, the racks achieve this through the opposite act of unfolding.

These works are shown alongside an architectural intervention, two layers of translucent fabric that cover the entire length of the gallery's curved glass window and visually interact with the hue of the ocean beyond. While the Binakul pattern in the main space creates a kind of visual 'interference' through optical illusion, the overlapping of the two layers here results in a moiré effect that Yang connects with the intersecting patterns in the now obsolete hyperbolic navigating systems that once helped ships at sea to determine their location.

Across the three galleries, *Strange Attractors* presents a complex synthesis of traditions and cultures, time periods and natural phenomena that are themselves varyingly concealed, latent or made evident. This is a universe that expands on Yang's existing interests and bodies of work, while bringing in distinctive ways of encountering her practice as we move across, and between, the spaces and relationships she has created.

The works that are unique to this exhibition, such as the *Sonic Intermediates* and *Non-Linear and Non-Periodic Dynamics*, become part of larger trajectories within Yang's practice that she sees as 'recurrent constellations' or 'incarnations' in terms of the forms and ideas that underpin them.[26] Just as Lorenz's strange attractors never retrace their movements, or close in on themselves, Yang's work charts a path that is constantly evolving.

1 Lorenz, a meteorologist at Massachusetts Institute of Technology, presented a paper entitled 'Does the flap of a butterfly's wings in Brazil set off a tornado in Texas?' at the 139th meeting of the American Association for the Advancement of Science, Washington D.C., December 1972. For an examination of the history and usage of the term 'butterfly effect' see Robert C. Hilborn, 'Sea gulls, butterflies, and grasshoppers: A brief history of the butterfly effect in nonlinear dynamics', *American Journal of Physics*, vol.72, no.4, 2004, pp.425–7, and Kevin Dooley, 'The Butterfly Effect of the "Butterfly Effect"' in *Nonlinear Dynamics, Psychology, and Life Sciences*, no.13, Aug. 2009, pp.279–88.

2 The articles in the previous note discuss some examples of literature and film that predate the actual identification of 'chaos theory' and the 'butterfly effect' in science. Notable among these is Ray Bradbury's short story 'A Sound of Thunder' (1952), which describes the unanticipated effect on the future that takes place when a man travels back in time and coincidentally steps on a butterfly.

3 '*Binakul* is a textile pattern handwoven on a small scale in Ilocos. Also known as *binakel*, *binakael*, or *binakol*, *binakul* (meaning 'twill' in Ilocano) is a variation of the *abel* [textile]. *Binakul* can be easily recognized by its uniform, interlocked geometric patterns that result in psychedelic optical art designs, which are said to represent the waves of the sea and, among indigenous peoples of the Cordilleras, protection against malevolent spirits.' See 'Art of the Loom: Weaving the Story that is the Binakul', Dec. 2013, https://yuchengcomuseum.org/art-loom-weaving-story-binakul, accessed 10 July 2020.

4 Chus Martínez, 'Nature Loves to Hide' in *Haegue Yang: ETA 1994–2018*, exh. cat., Museum Ludwig, Cologne 2018, p.6.

5 Having moved independently from London, Hepworth and Gabo both became part of an artists' enclave in St Ives. While Gabo moved to the United States in 1946, Hepworth lived and worked in St Ives for the rest of her life.

6 Li limited his palette to four colours: black for origin and end, red for blood and life, gold for nobility and white for purity.

7 See Hammad Nasar, 'Co-habiting New Worlds: The "Strange Attractions" of Li Yuan-chia', pp.11–15.

8 Diana Yeh, 'Under the Spectre of Orientalism and Nation: Translocal Crossings and Discrepant Modernities', in Michelle Ying-Ling Huang (ed.), *The Reception of Chinese Art across Cultures*, Newcastle upon Tyne 2014, pp.228–54.

9 Interestingly, another series of work where Yang's sculptures more closely resembled the forms of initial reference points were her *Sonic Figures* in the installation *Boxing Ballet* 2013–15. These took inspiration from Oskar Schlemmer's *Triadic Ballet* (1922) which comprised three dancers, three acts, and three colours, with twelve choreographies and eighteen costumes.

10 The work was based around the unconventional companionship of Marguerite Duras, Robert Antelme and Dionys Mascolo during the French Resistance. See *Haegue Yang: Lingering Nous*, exh. cat., Centre Pompidou, Paris 2017, p.60.

11 Haegue Yang in Nadine Khalil, 'All That Noise', *A Magazine*, no.87, Feb. 2017, p.213.

12 Leonie Radine, 'About Haegue Yang', in *Haegue Yang: ETA 1994–2018*, p.398.

13 Doryun Chong, 'A Less Small Dictionary (for HY)', in Bruna Roccasalva (ed.), *Haegue Yang Anthology 2006–2018: Tightrope Walking and Its Wordless Shadow*, Milan 2019, p.117.

14 This shape was also a primary element in Yang's exhibition *Handles* at the Museum of Modern Art in New York (2019–20).

15 George Ivanovich Gurdjieff, *In Search of Being: The Fourth Way to Consciousness*, ed. Steven A. Grant, Boston and London 2012, p.242.

16 Stuart Comer, 'The Mystic Landscapes of Haegue Yang', *Museum of Modern Art Magazine*, 25 Oct. 2019, https://www.moma.org/magazine/articles/167, accessed 10 July 2020.

17 Ibid.

18 Ibid.

19 *The Seventh Continent*, 16th Istanbul Biennial, curated by Nicolas Bourriaud, 14 Sept.–10 Nov. 2019. The wallpaper work was originally developed for *Chronotopic Traverses,* La Panacée-MO.CO, Montpellier, 12 Oct. 2018–13 Jan. 2019 and adapted for the Istanbul Biennial.

20 *In the Cone of Uncertainty*, The Bass, Miami Beach, Florida, 2 Nov. 2019–5 April 2020.

21 These are part of a larger series of works, *Non-Foldings*, that was made from 2007–15.

22 'I went there and the drying rack, IV drip, fans, strobes and origami – they were all there – and it all just came together in my work...' Haegue Yang in Khalil 2017, p.213.

23 'Traveling Voices, A Conversation between Haegue Yang and Yilmaz Dziewior', in *Haegue Yang: ETA 1994–2018*, p.364.

24 Yilmaz Dziewior, 'Arrived: Yilmaz Dziewior in conversation with Haegue Yang', in Roccasalva 2019, p.180.

25 Chong 2019, p.89.

26 'Traveling Voices, A Conversation between Haegue Yang and Yilmaz Dziewior', p.354.

An example of the
Binakul textile pattern

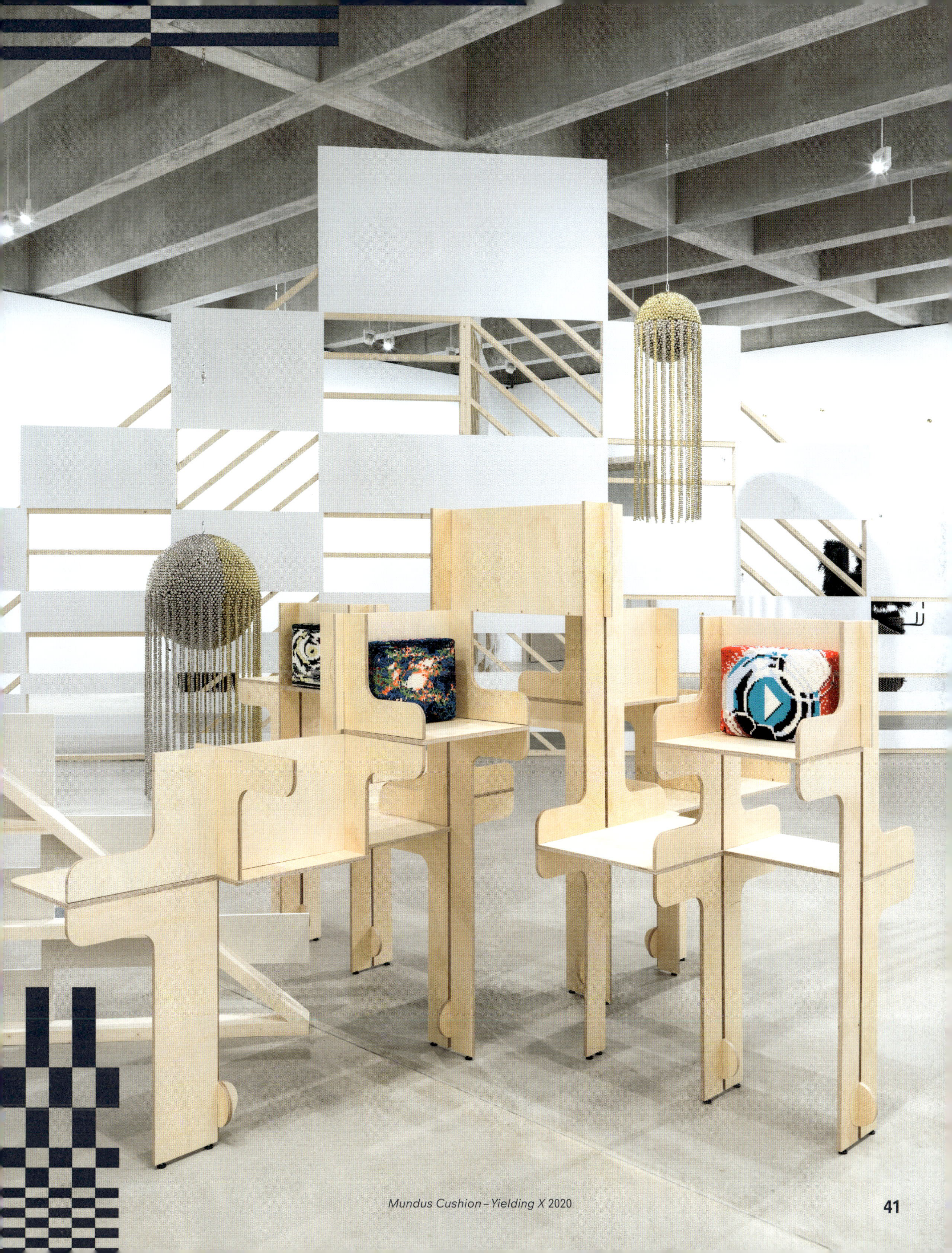

Mundus Cushion – Yielding X 2020

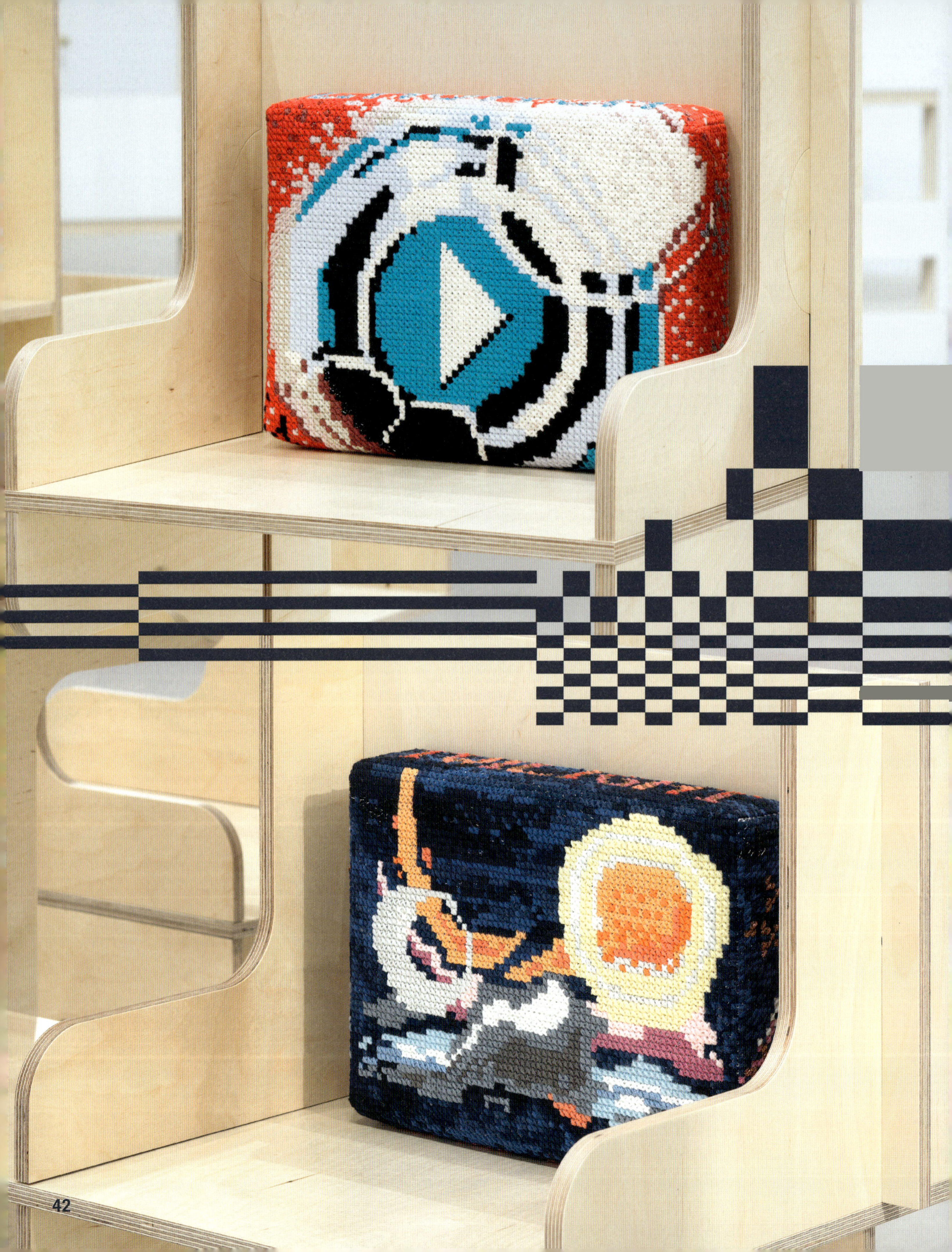

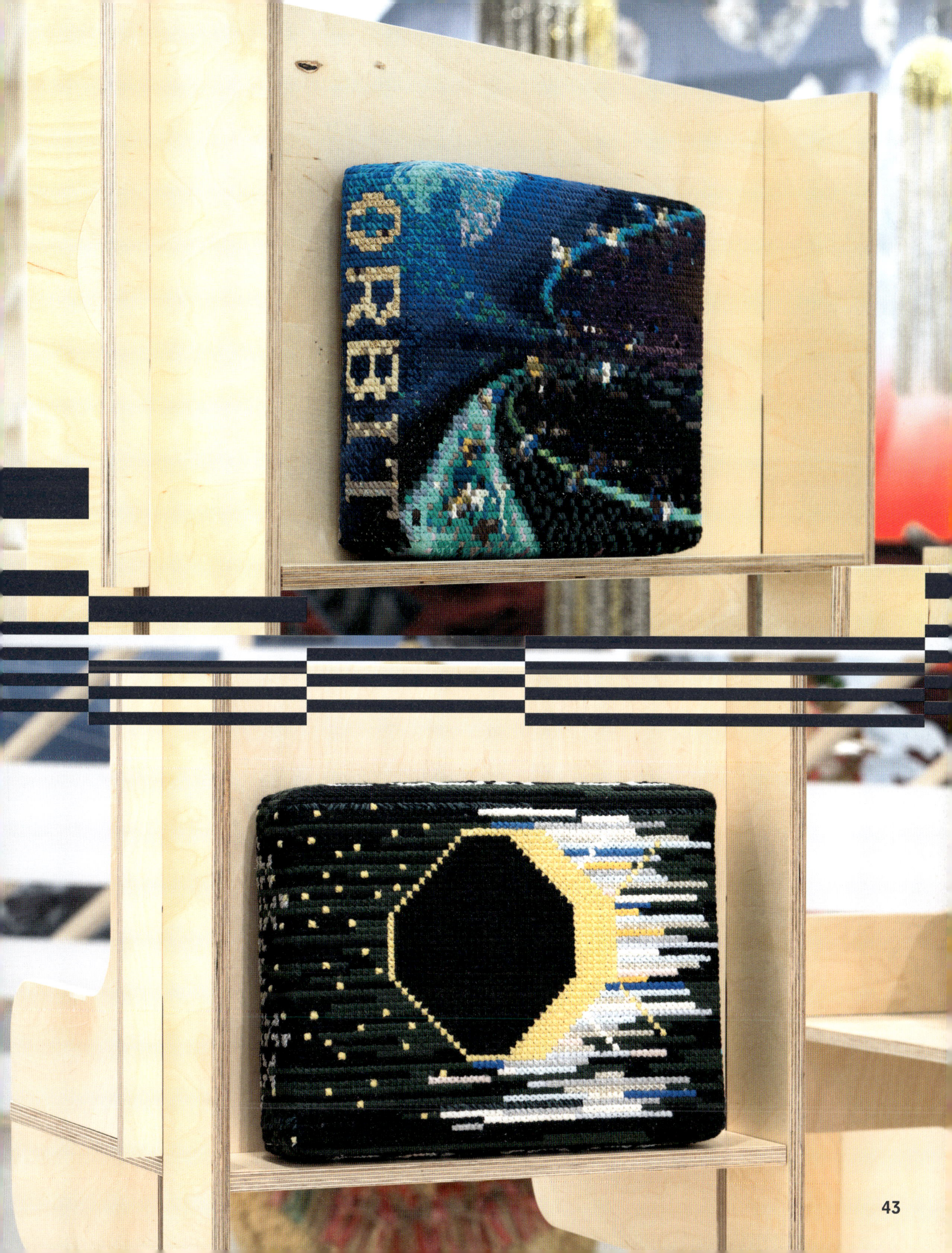
ORBIT

Fluidity on Nonagonal Crystal Matrix – Trustworthy #400 2020

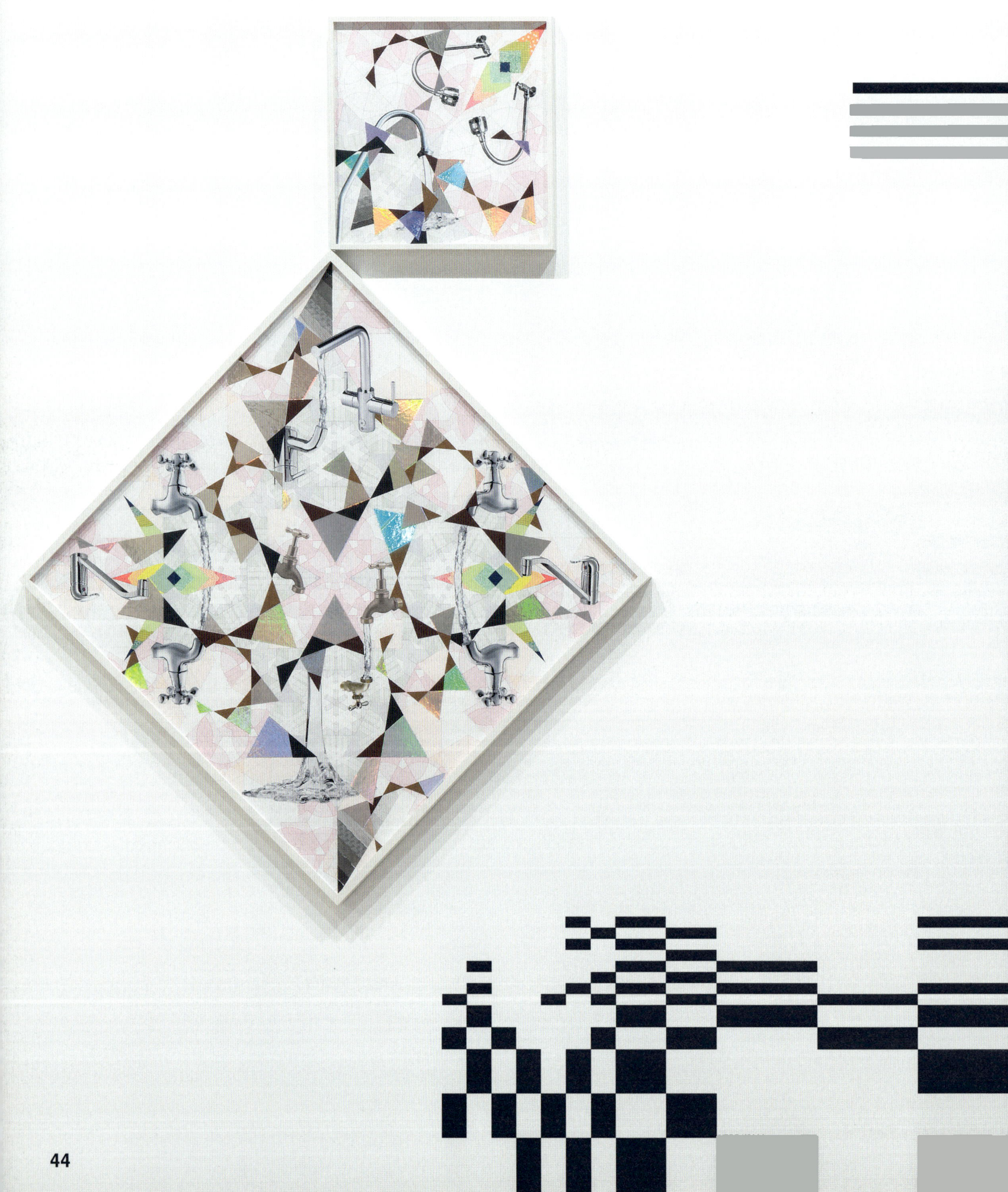

Cornish Healing Catch – Trustworthy #403 2020

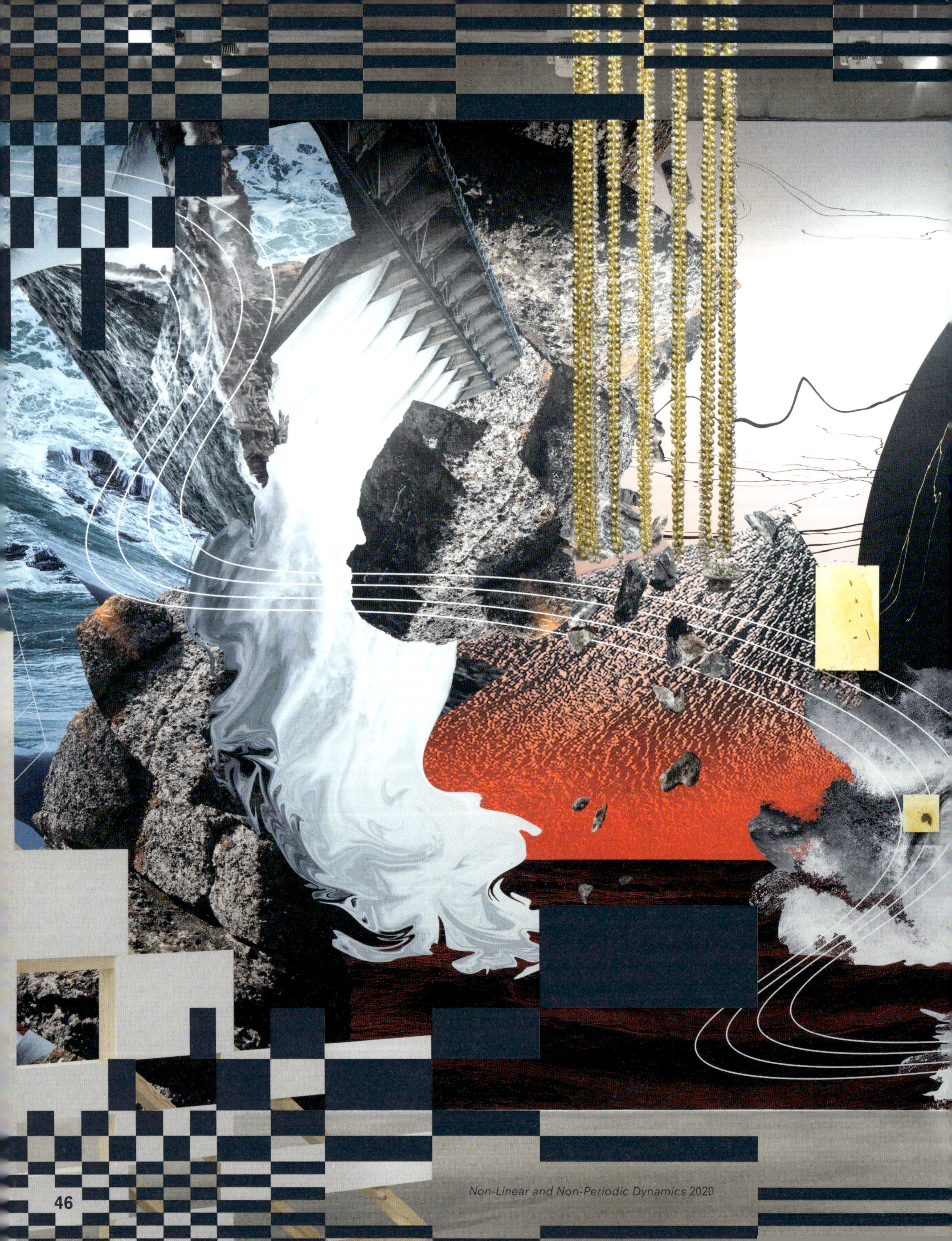

Non-Linear and Non-Periodic Dynamics 2020

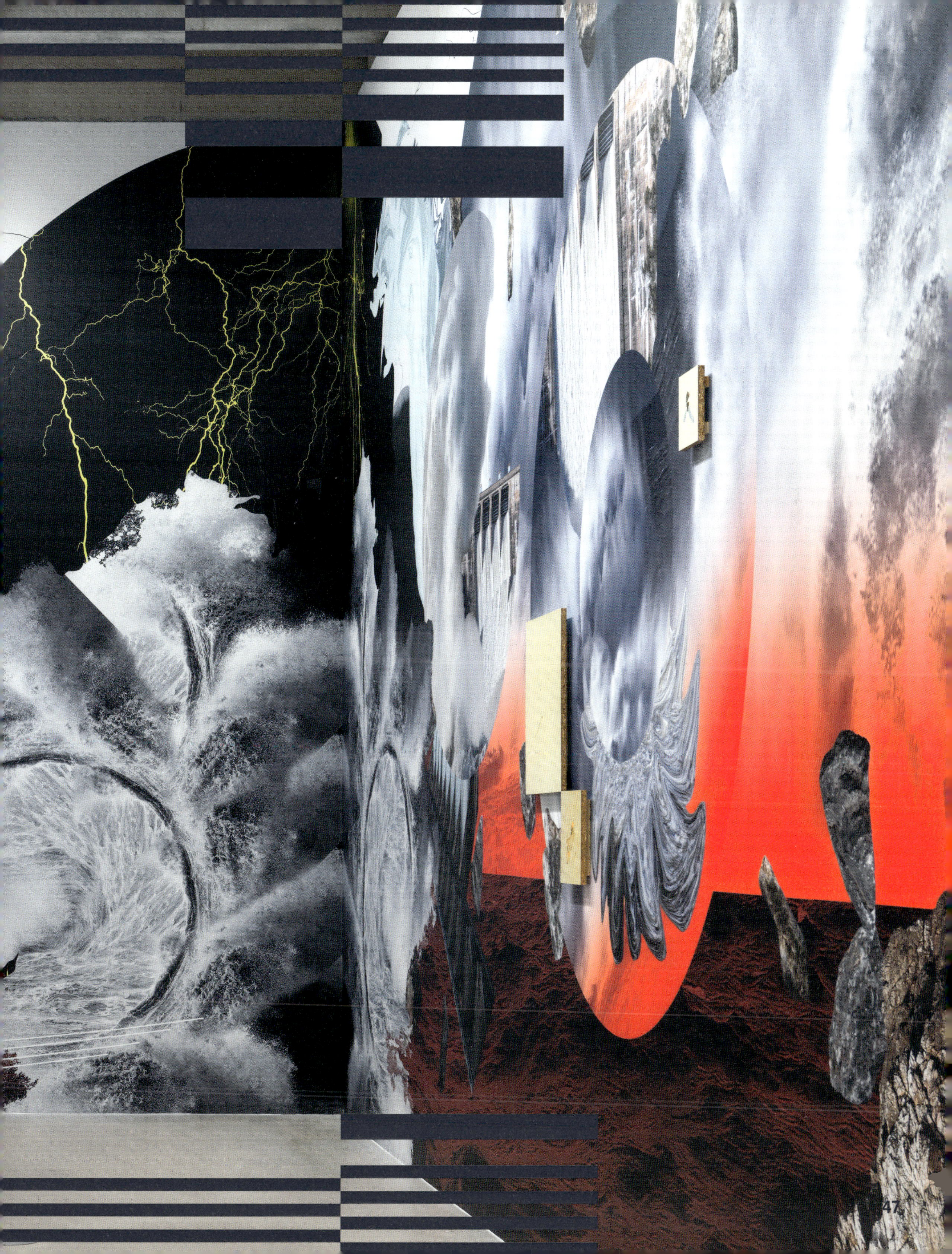

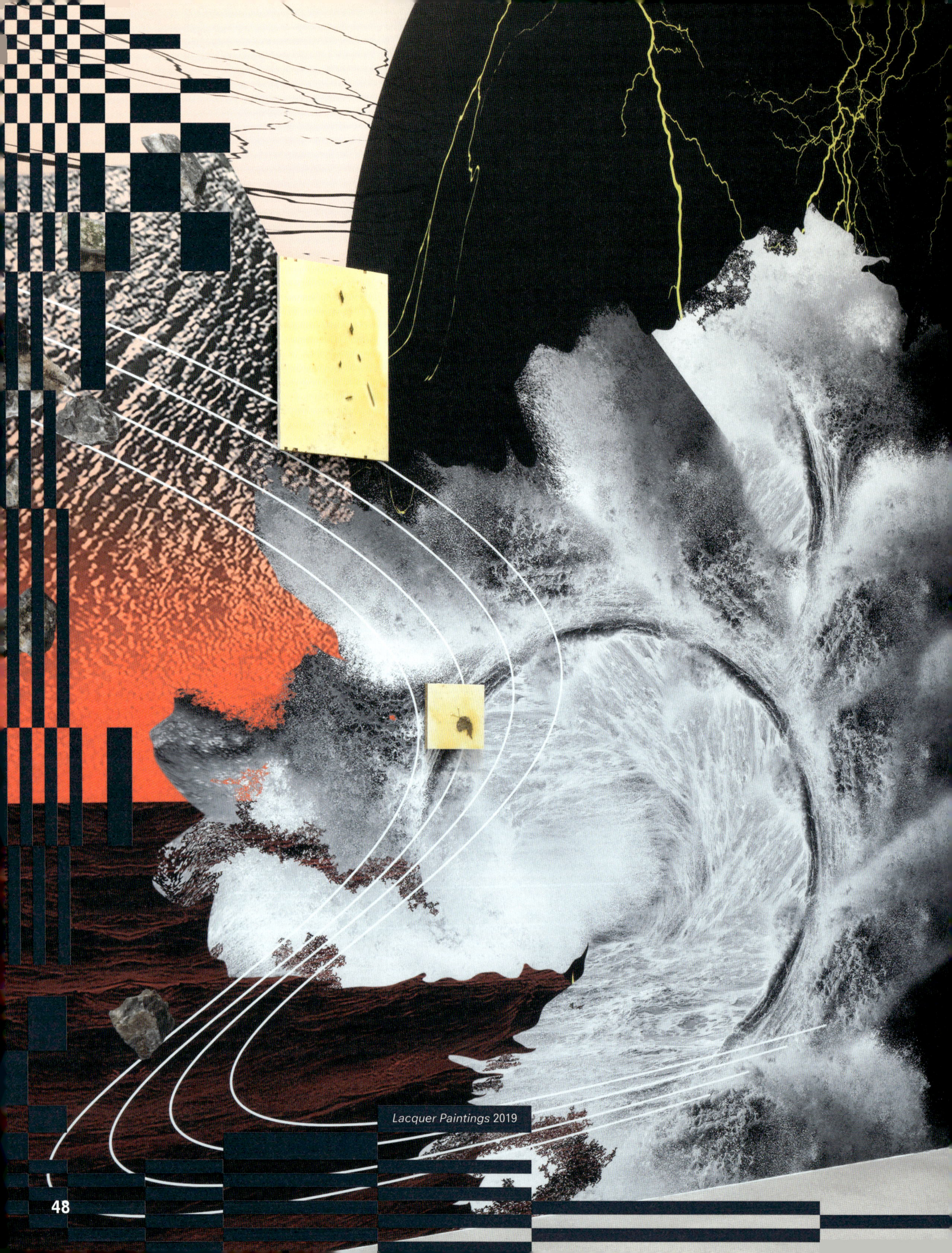

Lacquer Paintings 2019

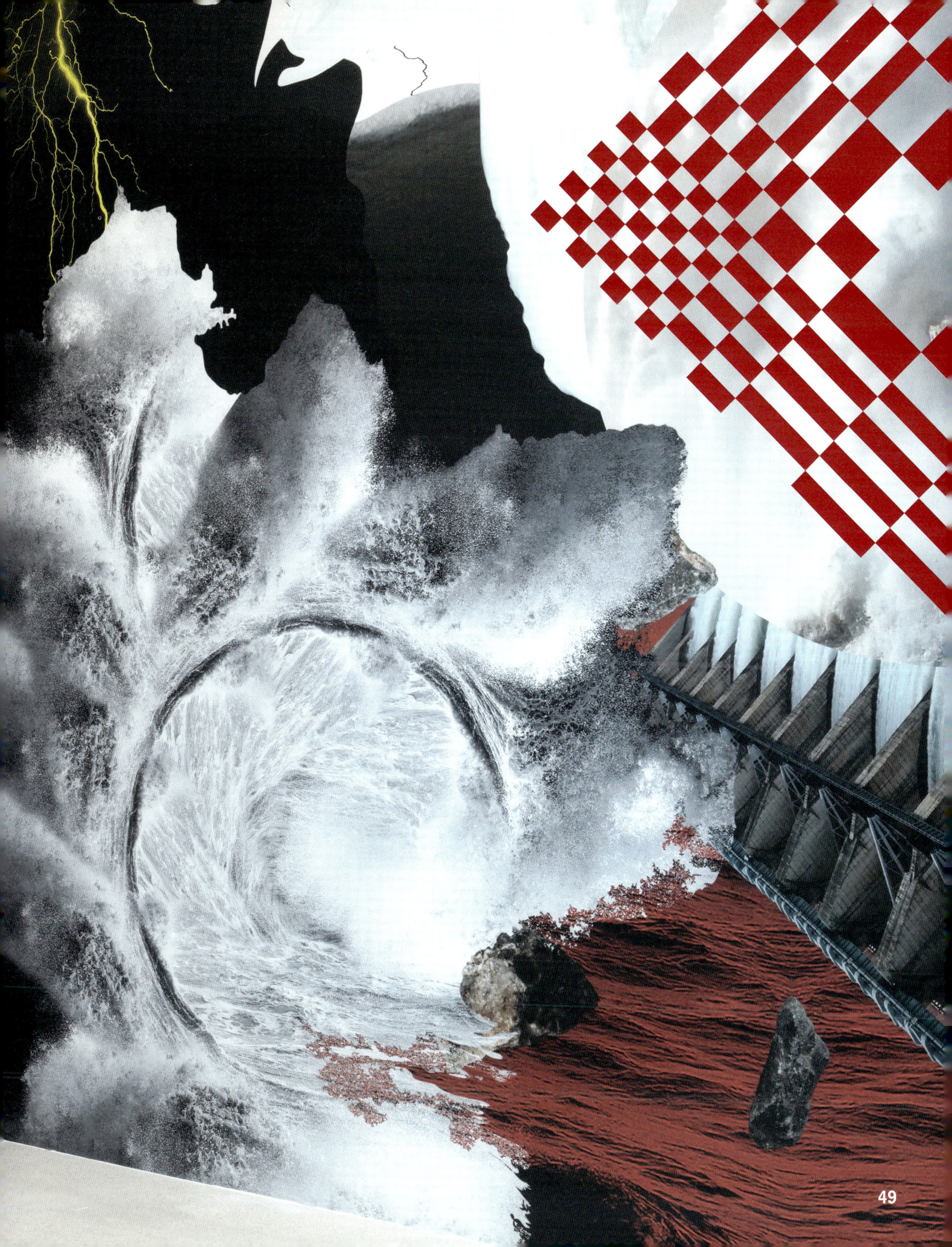

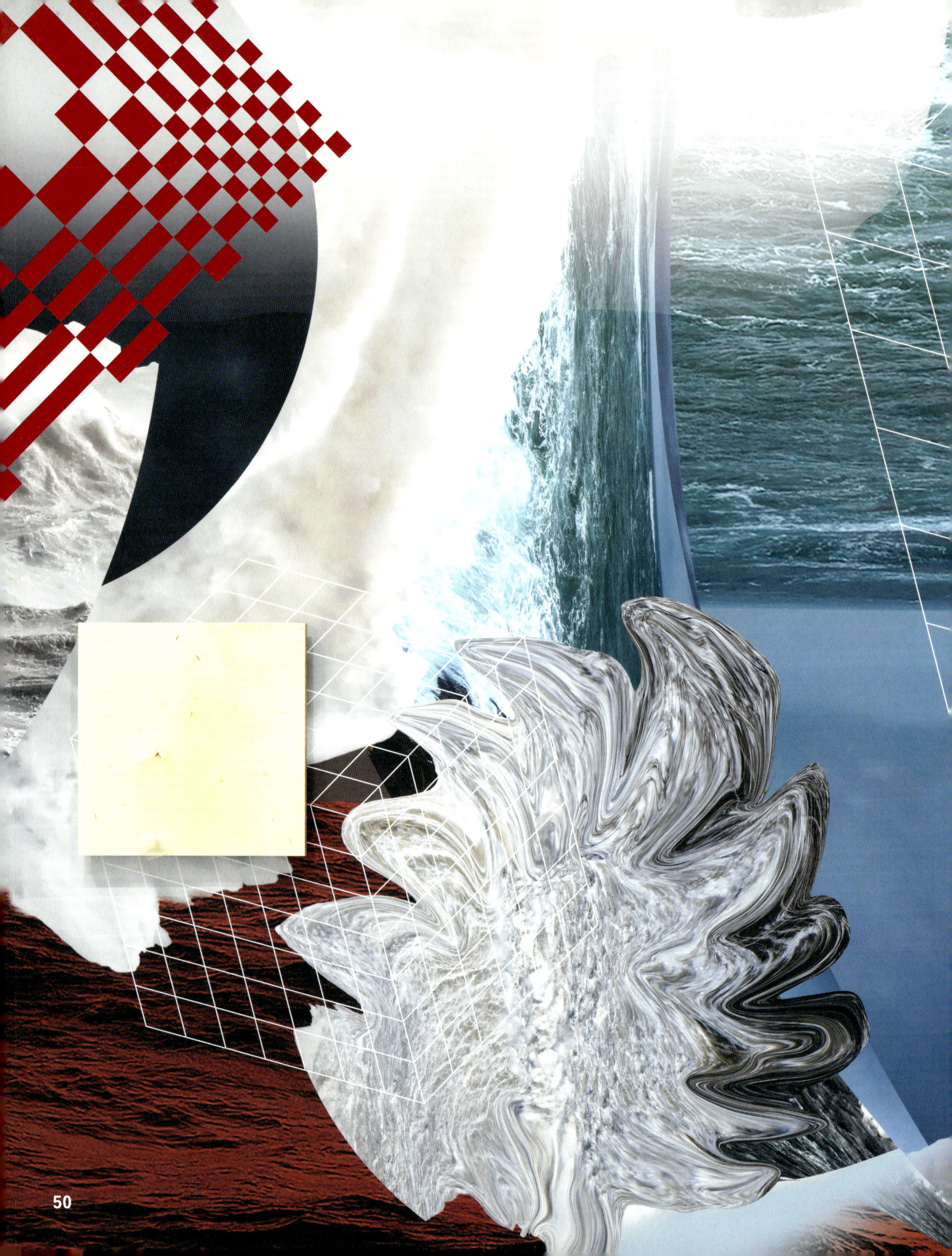

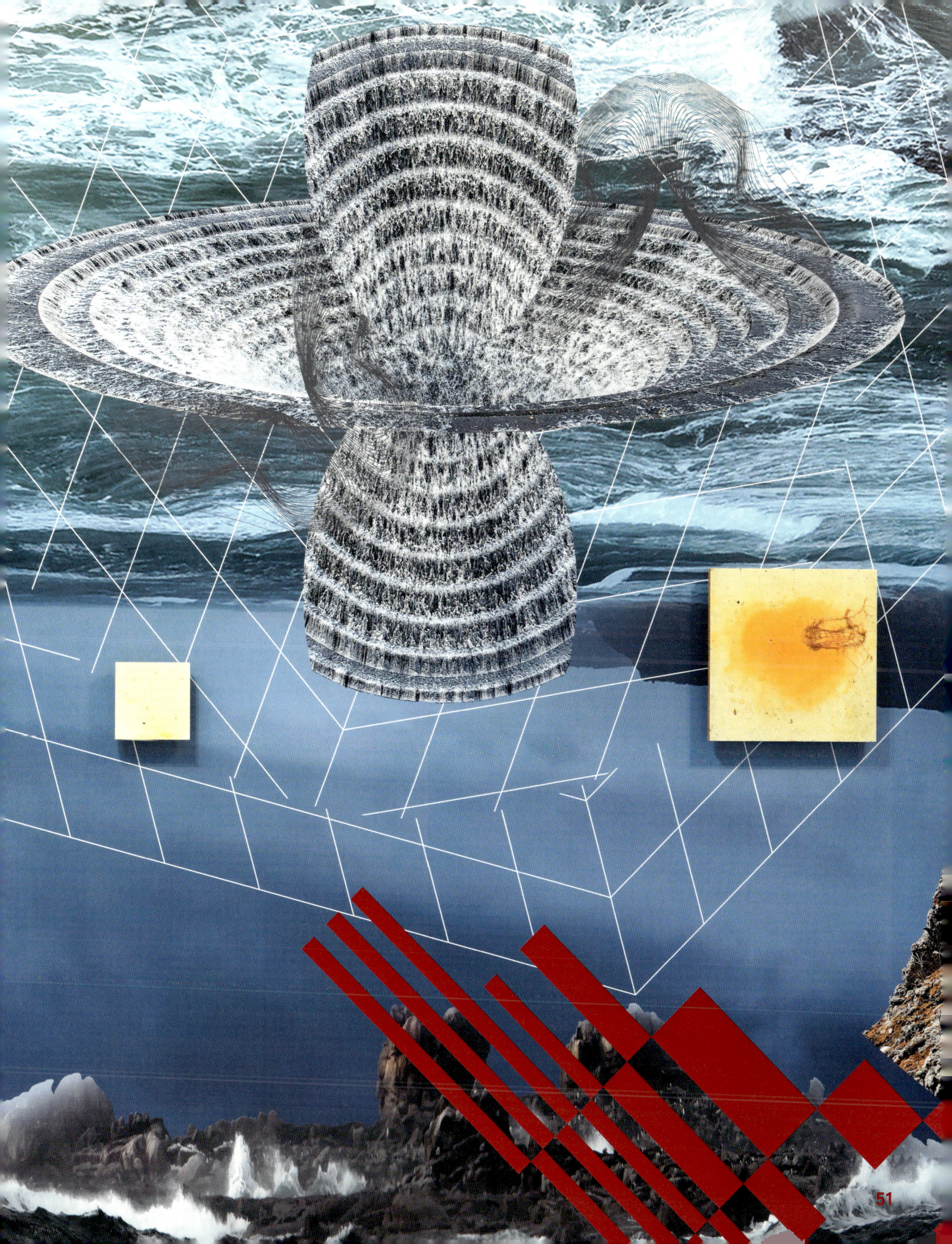

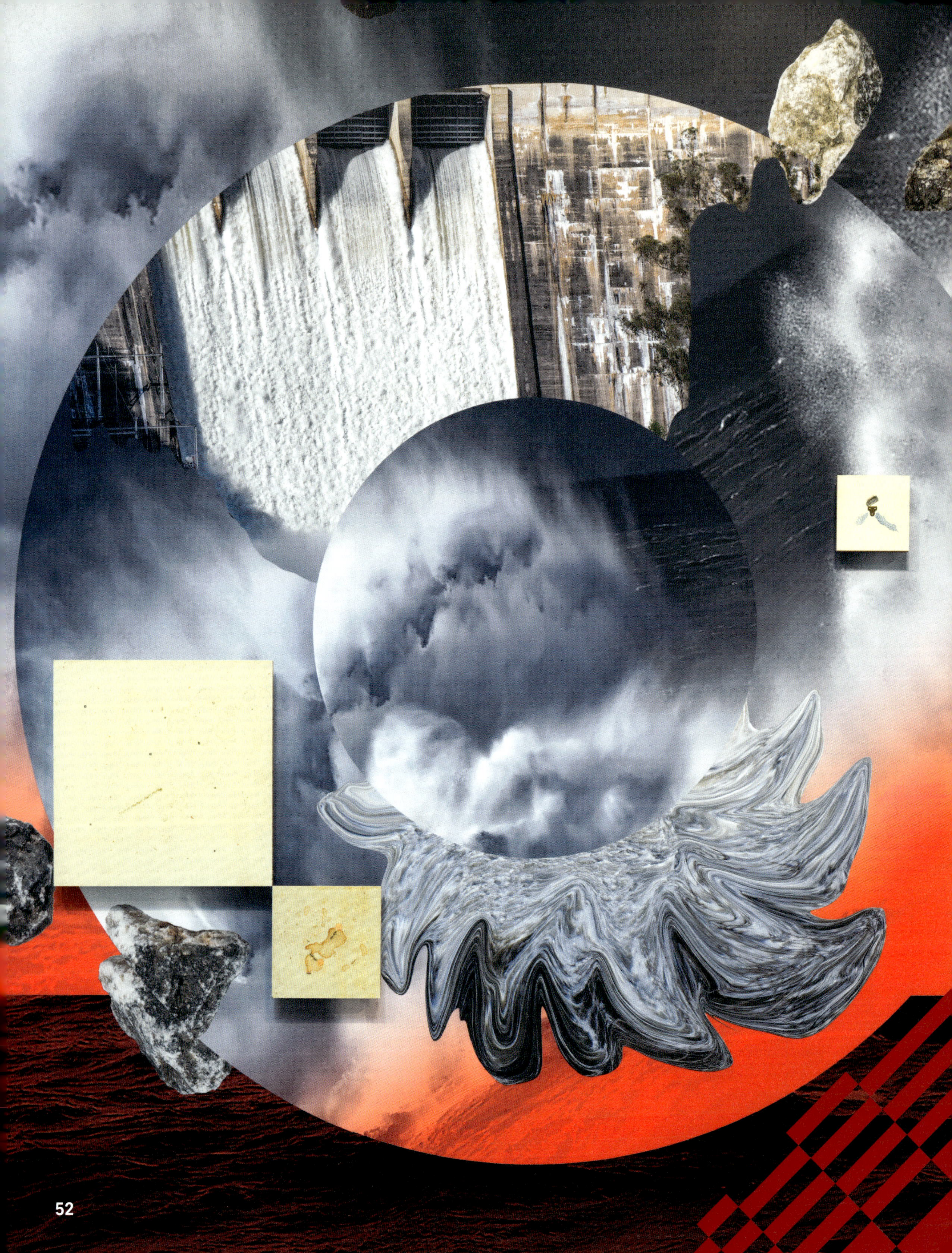

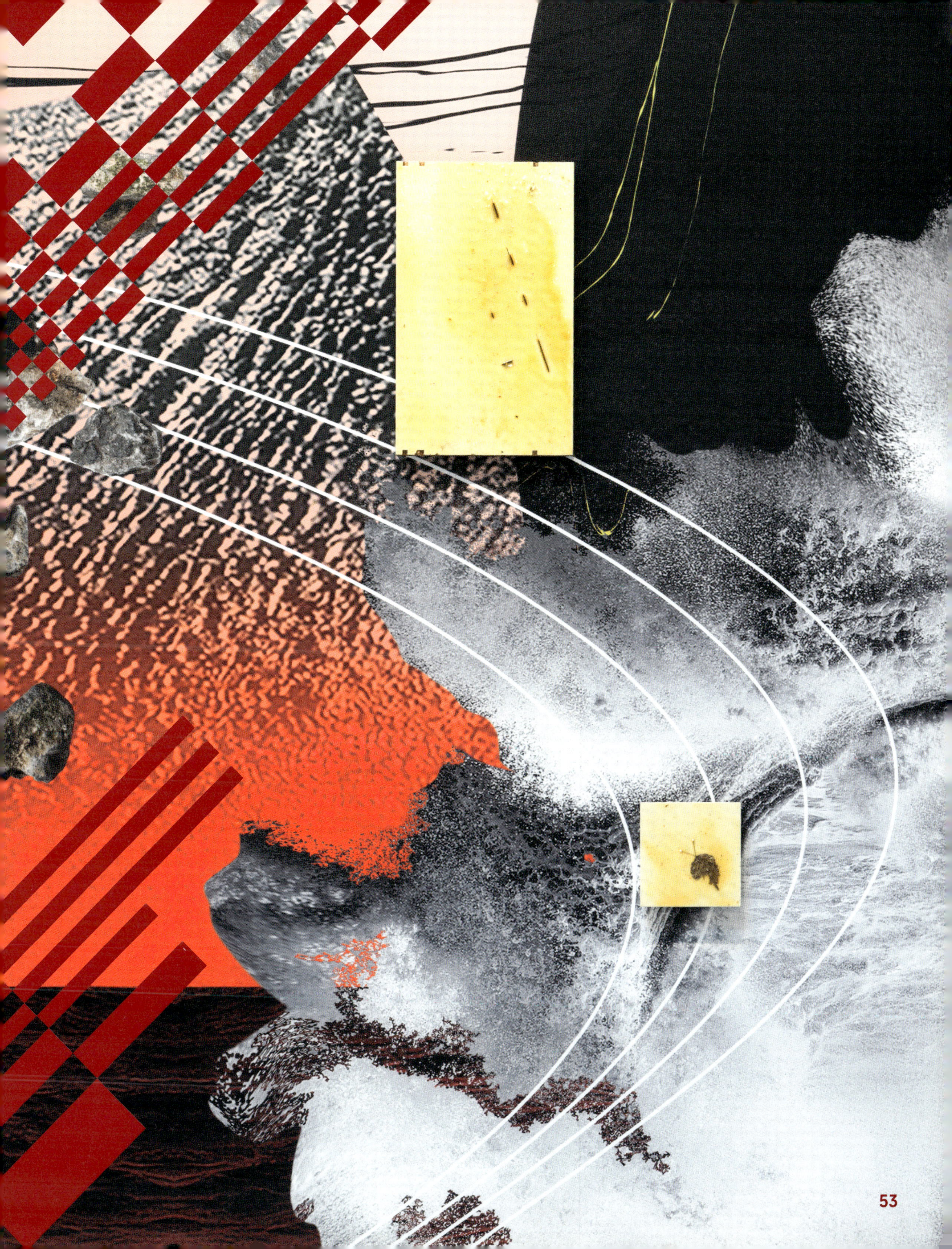

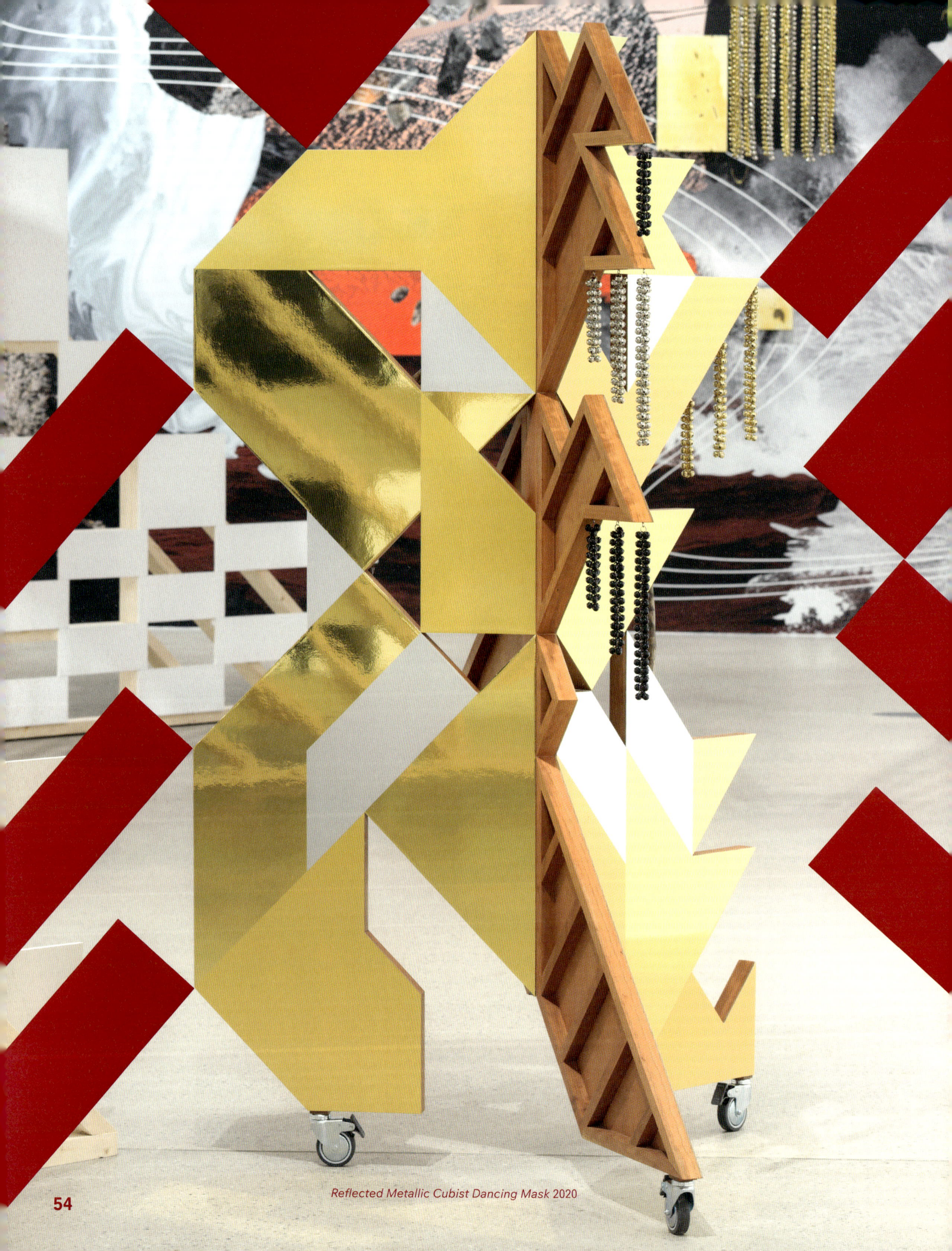

Reflected Metallic Cubist Dancing Mask 2020

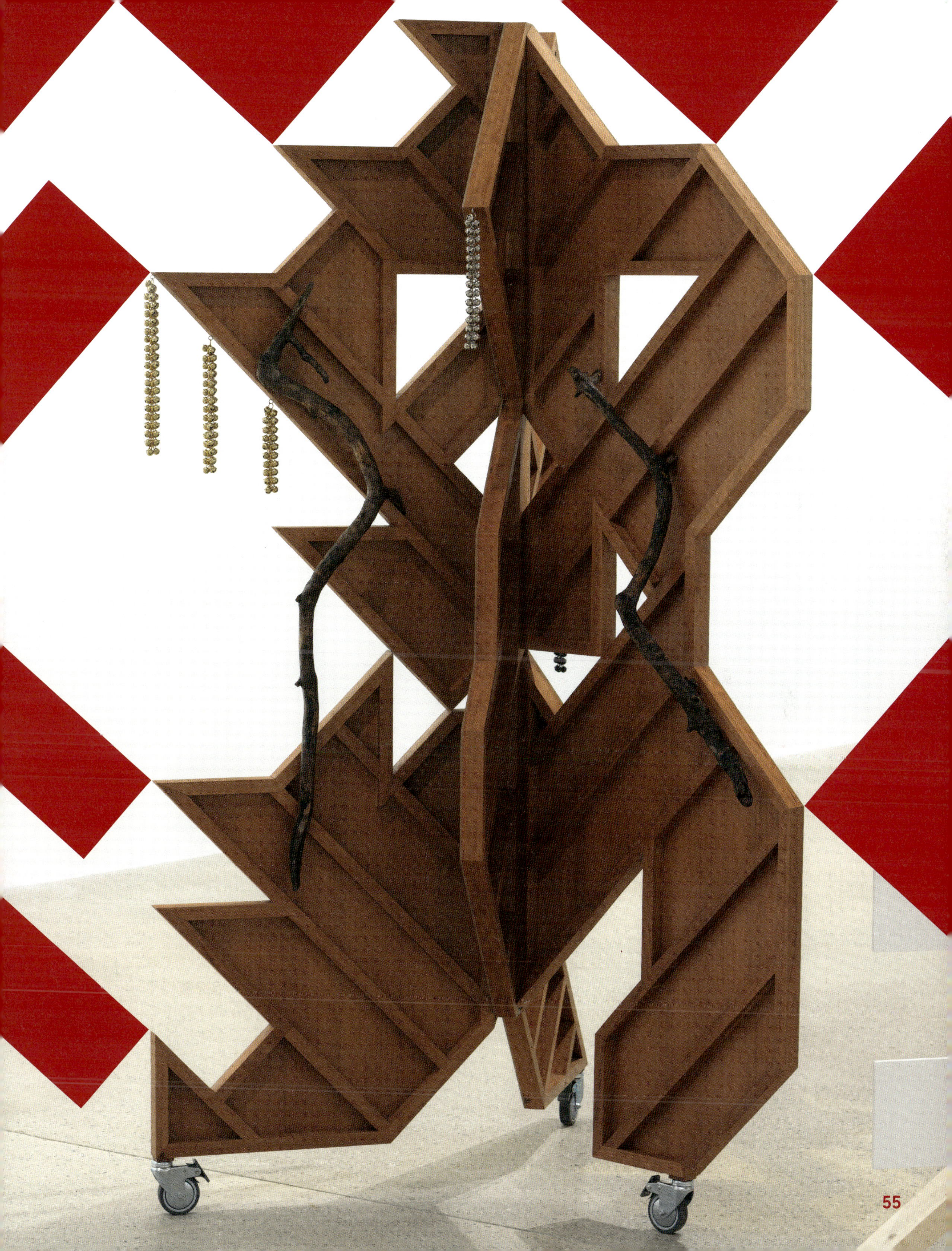

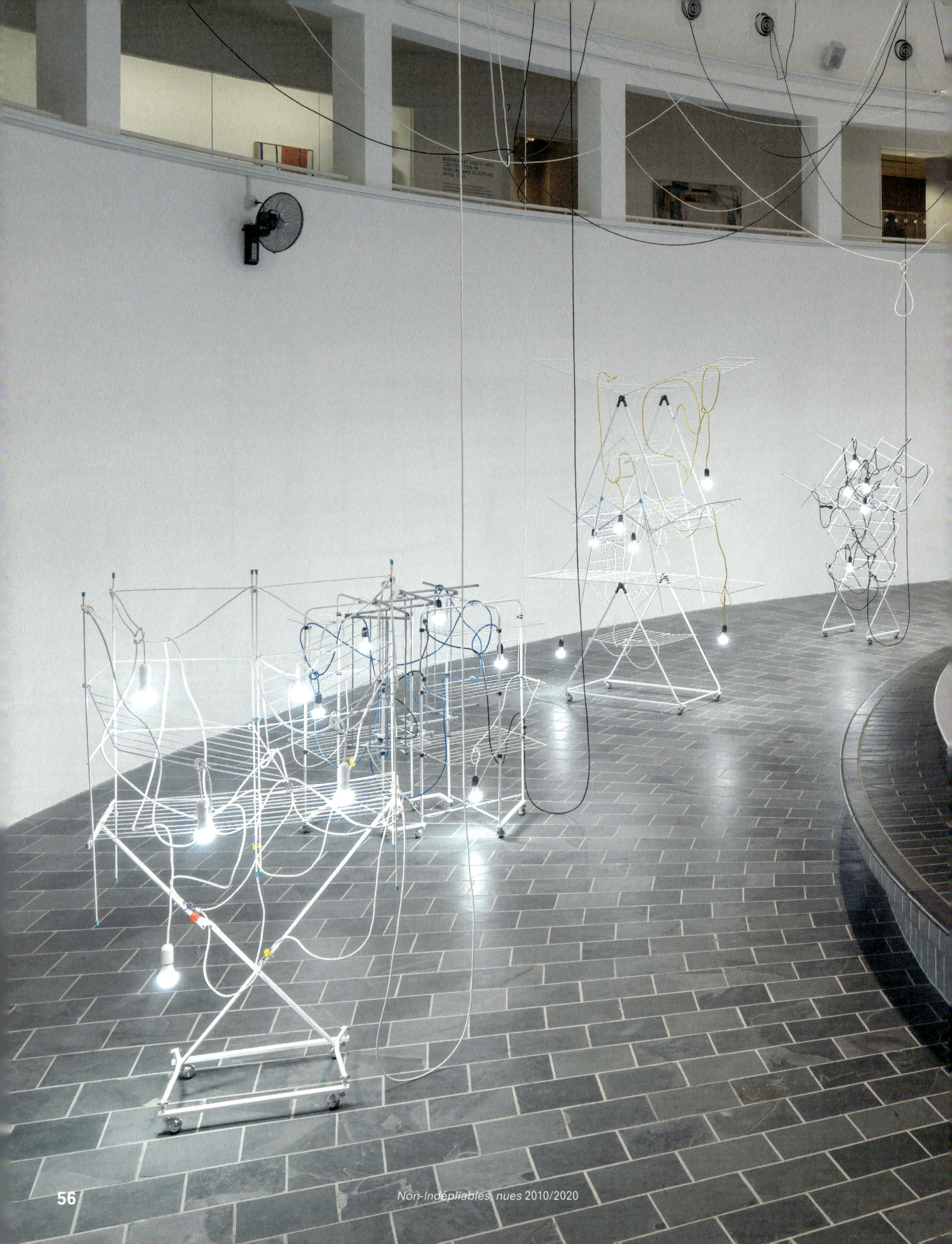

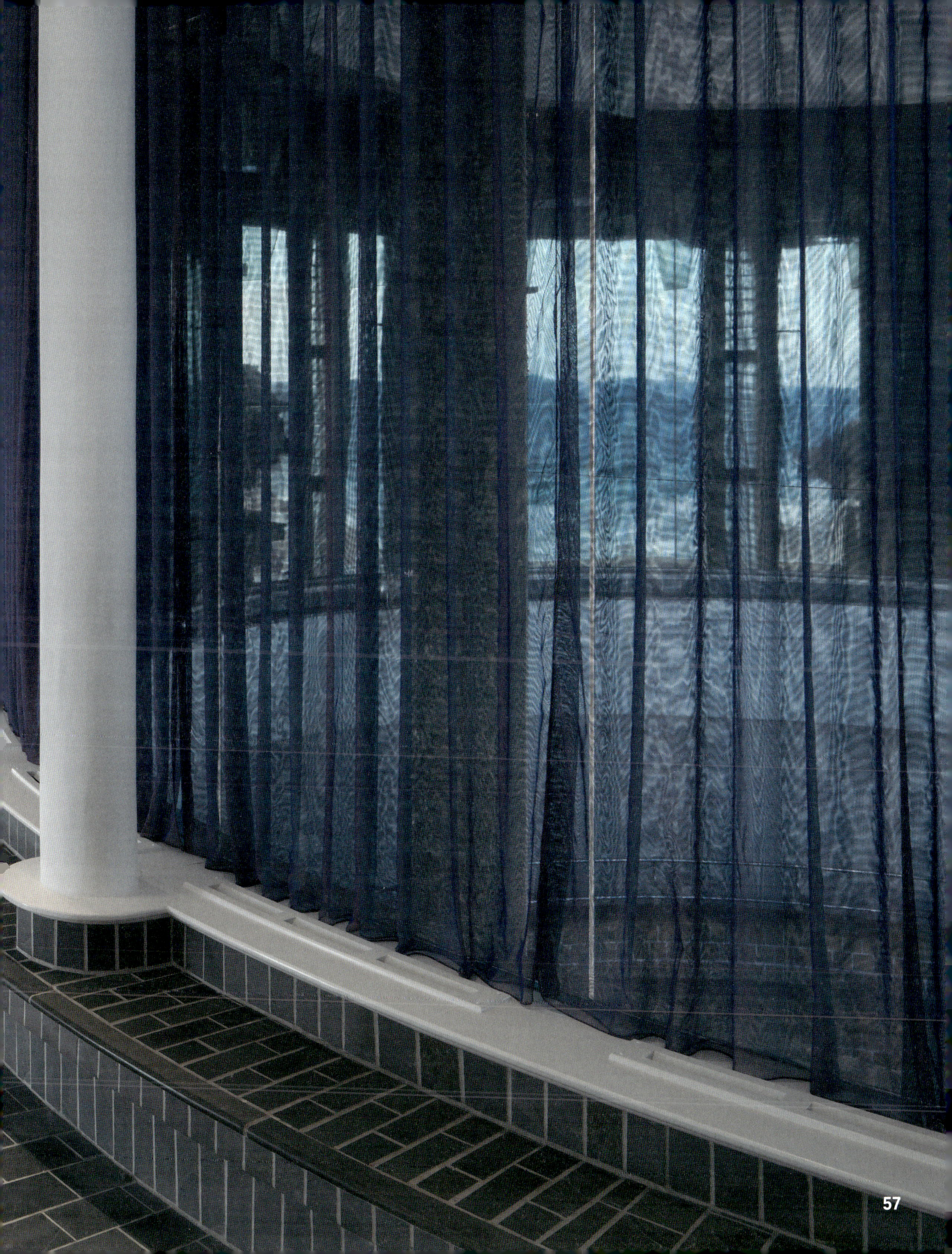

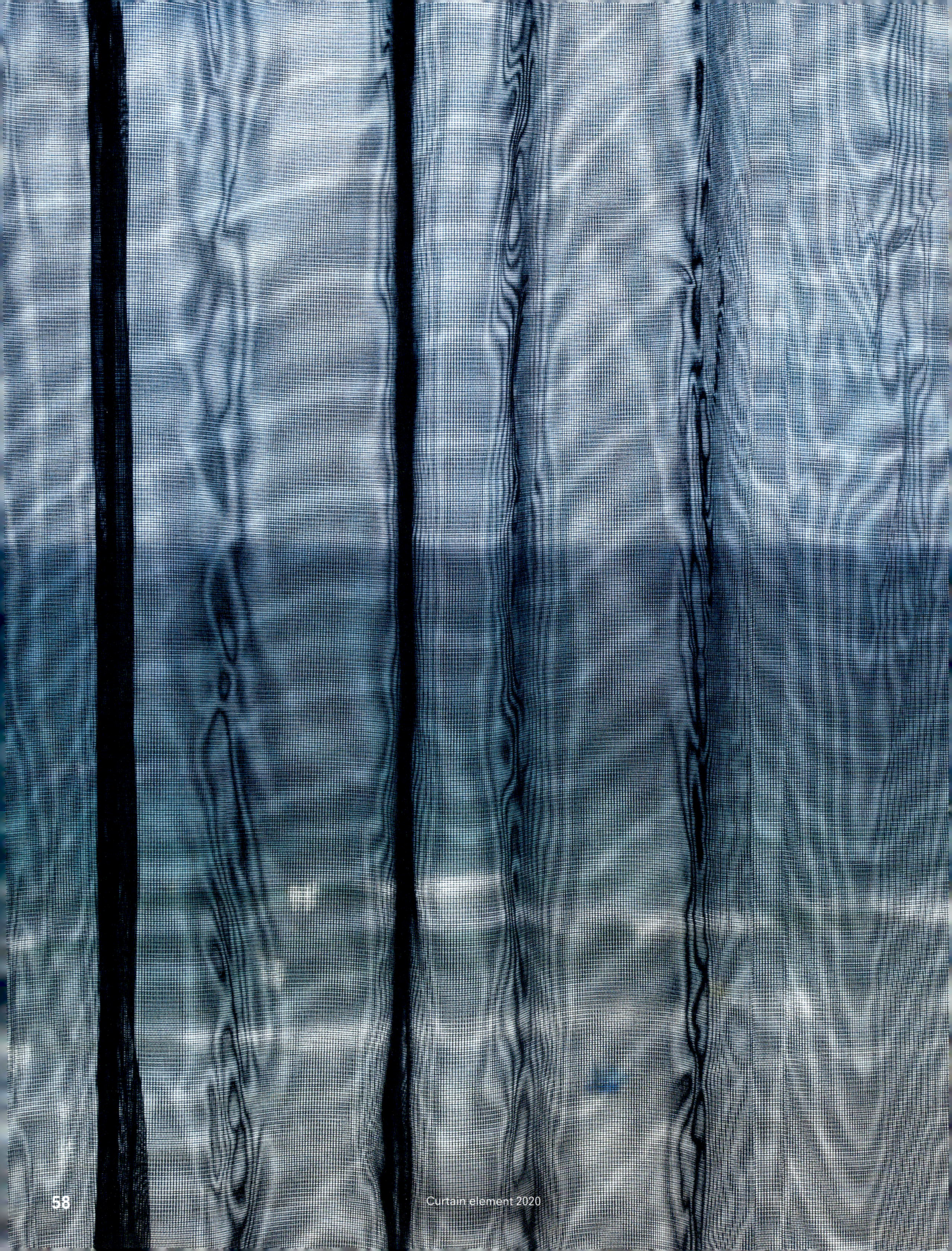

Curtain element 2020

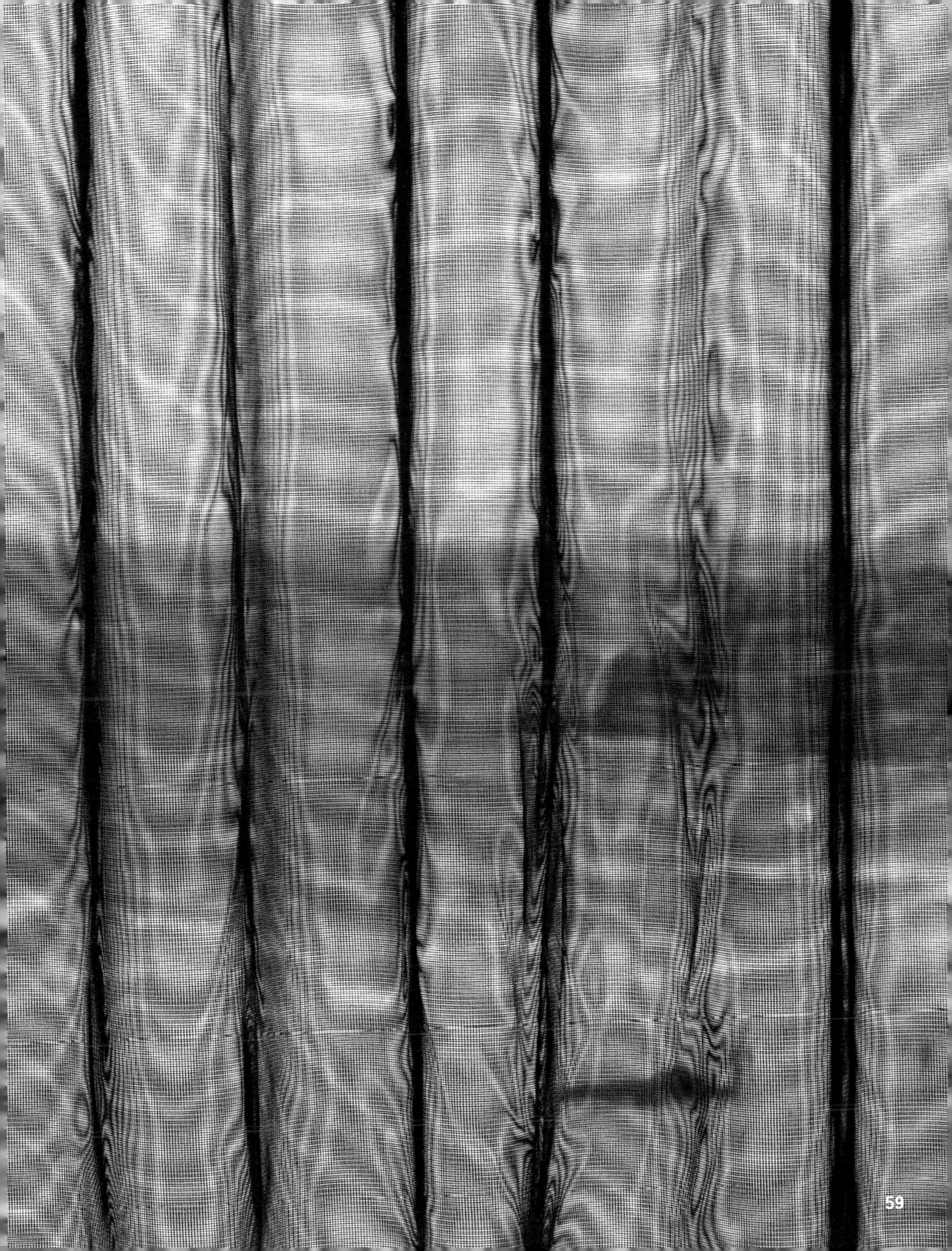

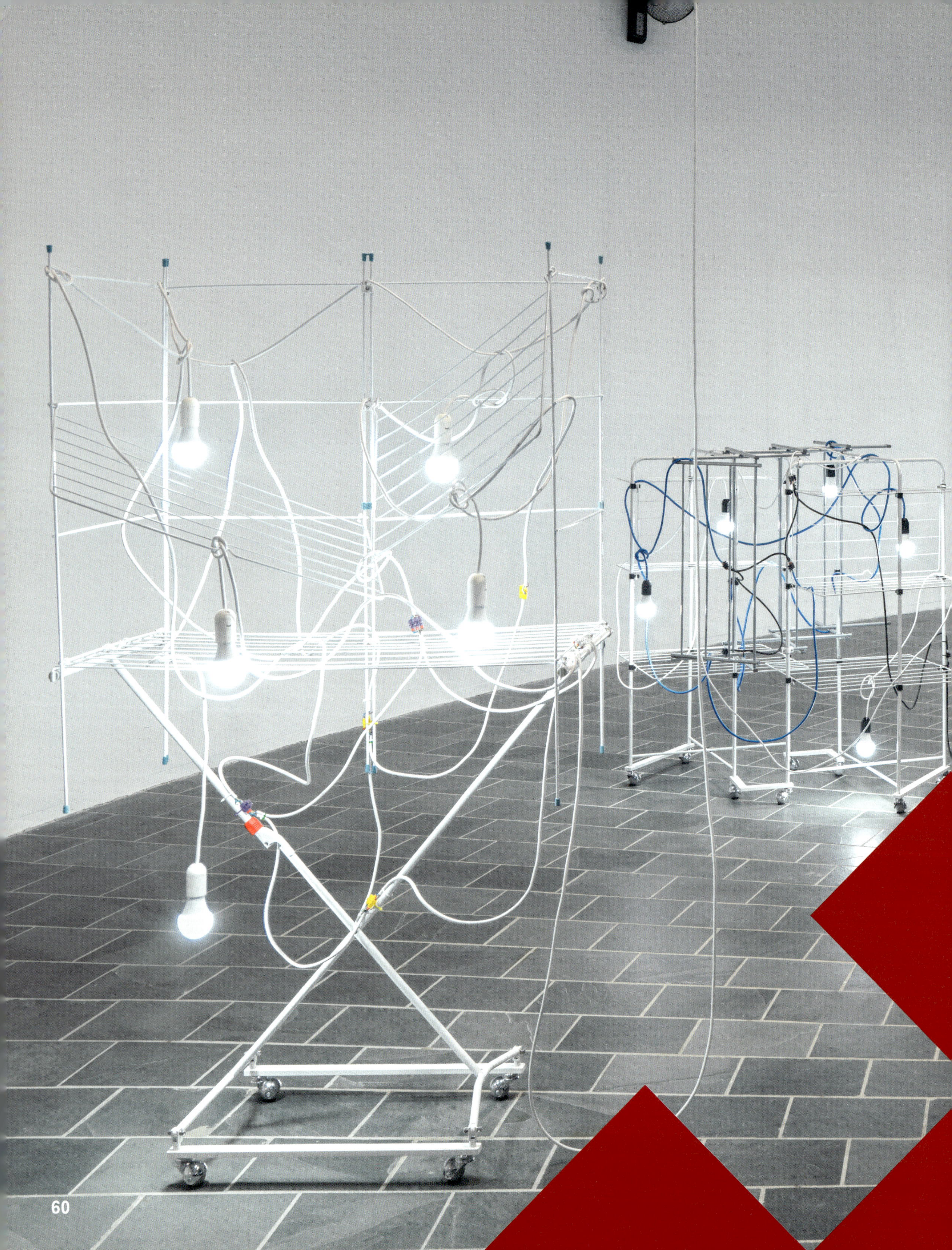

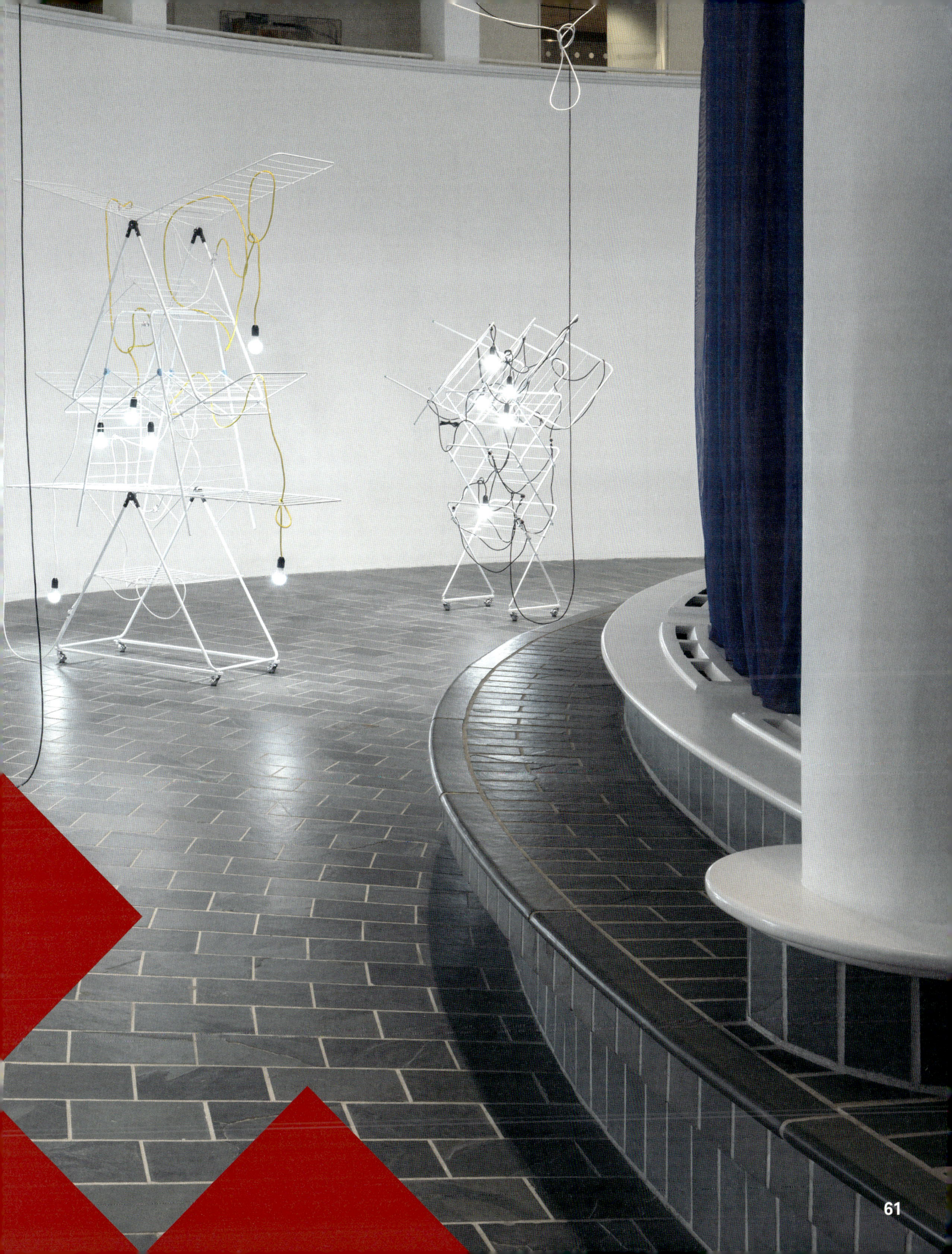

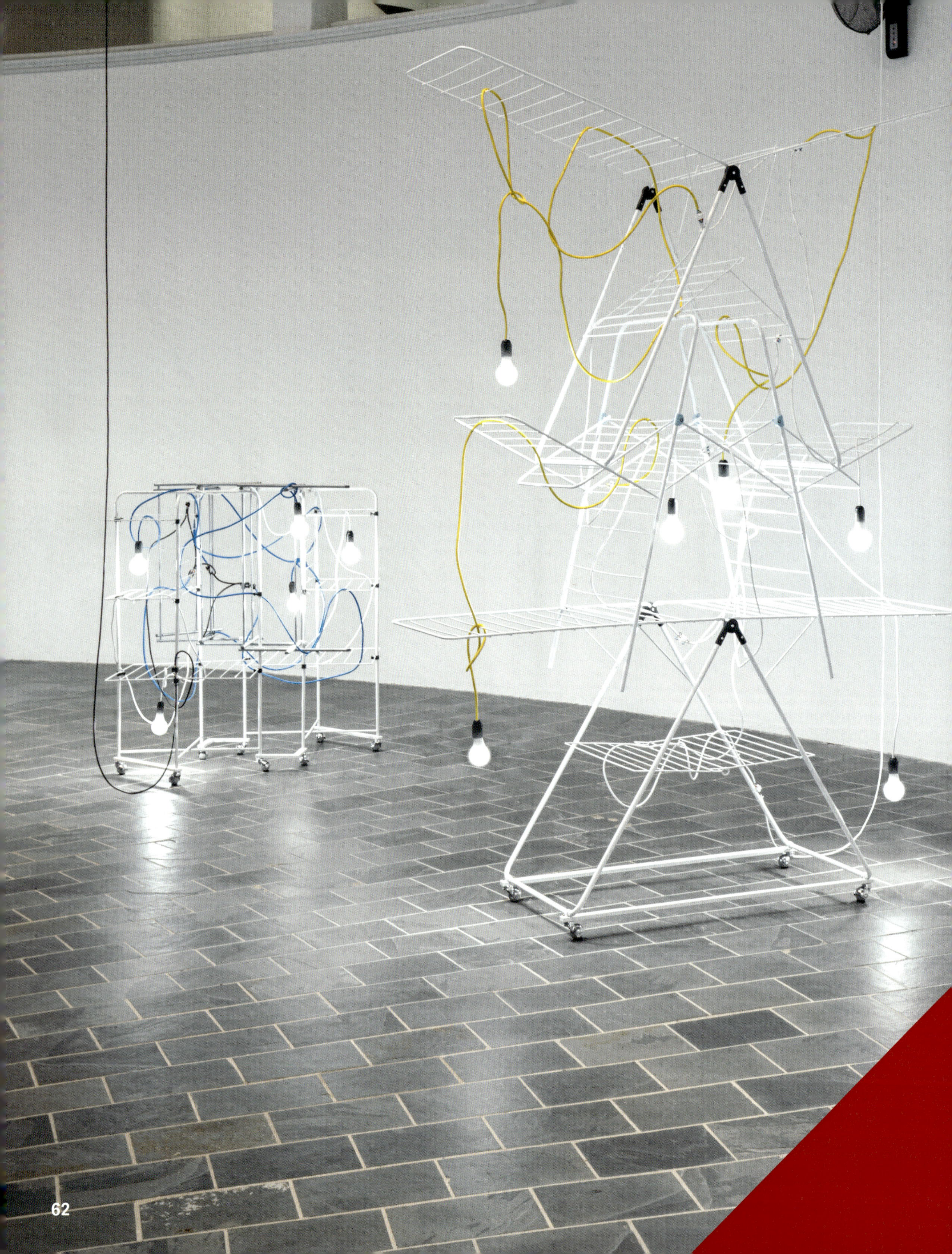

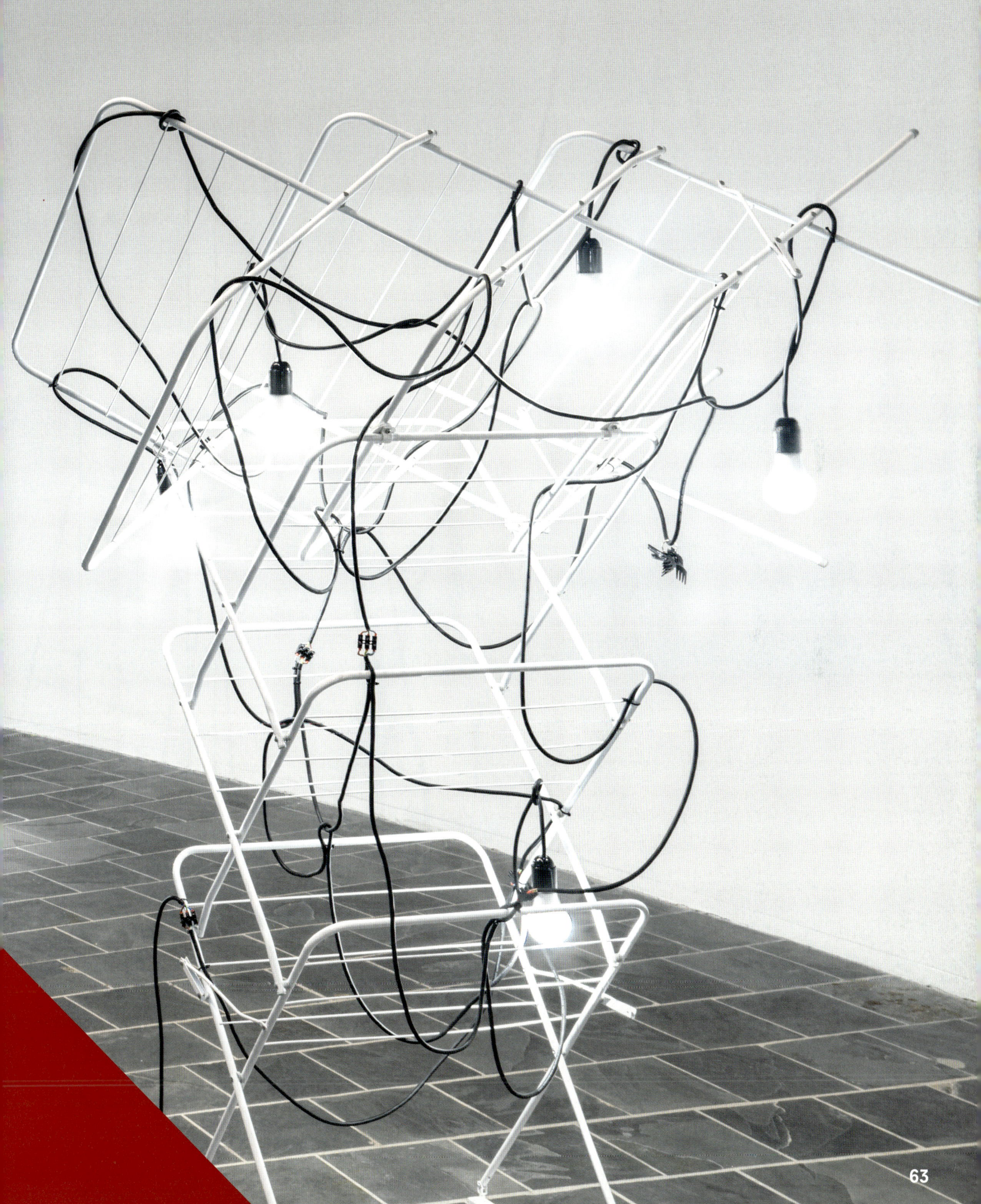

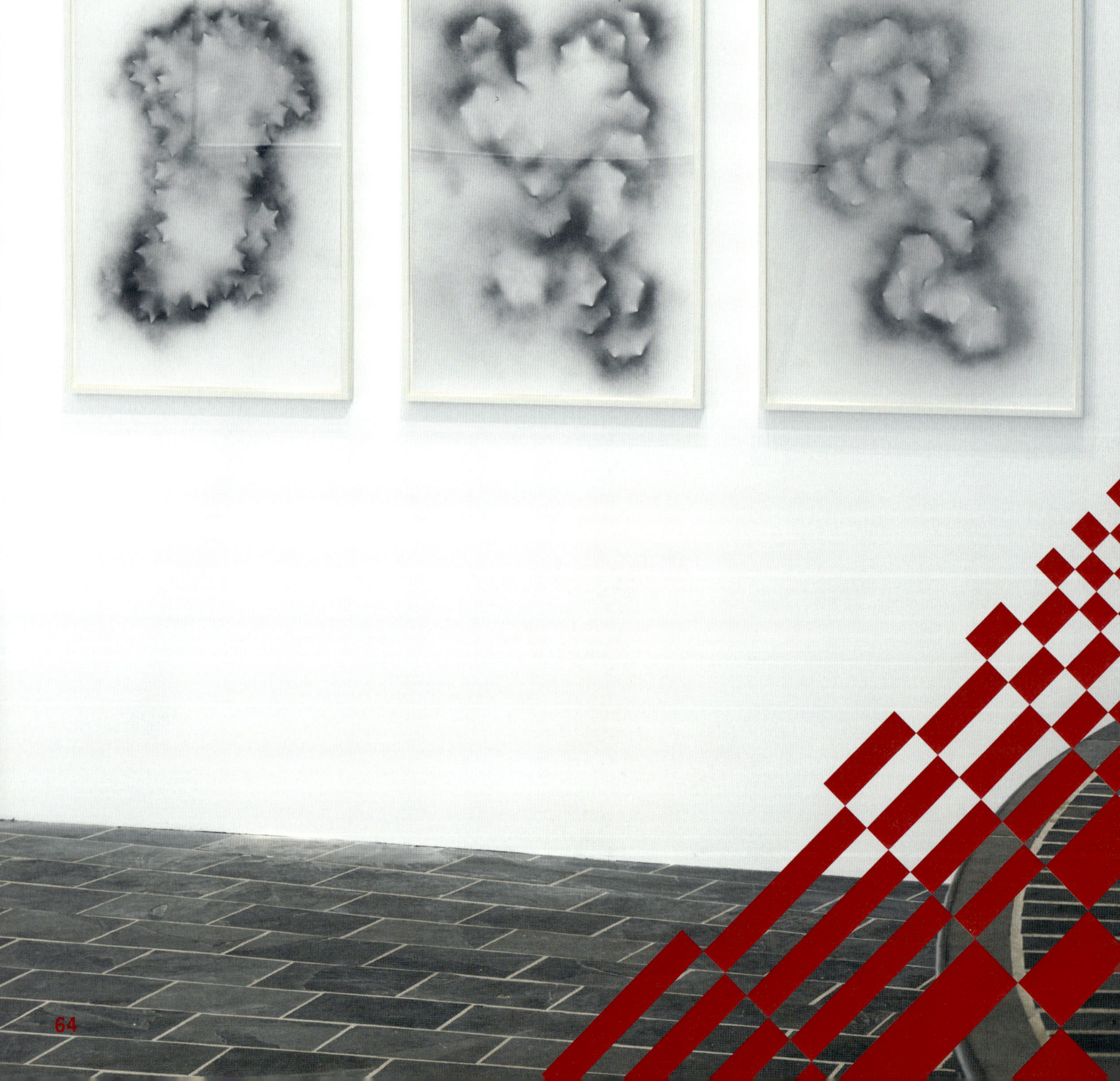

Chrono-Notes
From 'The Third Effort toward a Dictionary for Haegue Yang'

Compiled by Magdalen Chua
with Doryun Chong

Unknown
The maypole dance is a ceremonial folk dance around a tall pole that is often garlanded with flowers and woven ribbons. These dances date back to ancient spring and fertility rites of dancing around a tree and are now frequently performed on May Day (1 May) or midsummer in Scandinavia. Although typically associated with Western European traditions, similar dances are performed in India and in ritual dances in Latin America and the Basque Country.

37 BC–668 AD
The Tomb Murals of the Four Guardian Deities from Gangseojungmyo (the Middle Tomb of Gangseo) are vestiges of culture from the Goguryeo (37 BC–668 AD), an ancient kingdom that ruled parts of the Korean Peninsula and Manchuria. Gangseojungmyo is one of three royal tombs. Its four walls feature a pair of red phoenixes (south), a blue dragon (east), a white tiger (west), and a black tortoise-serpent (north), reflecting the Goguryeo people's belief in these deities as guardians of the four cardinal directions and protectors of a tomb. The ceiling, which is decorated with the lotus, sun and moon, is characteristic of Goguryeo mural tombs built before the 6th century.

3 BC–4 AD
The Classic of Mountains and Seas or *Shan Hai Jing* is a collection and source of ancient Chinese mythology. Divided into eighteen chapters, it depicts the rituals, medicine, animals, natural history and peoples of the ancient world. The descriptions – by turns mundane, fanciful and strange – are classified into four categories: 'Mountains', 'Regions Beyond the Seas', 'Regions within the Seas' and 'The Great Wilderness'. The classic is said to consist of accounts by different people, probably written from the Warring States (475 BC) to the Han dynasty (206 BC–220 AD).

1869
The novel *The Man Who Laughs* by French poet and novelist Victor Hugo (1802–85) is first published under the French title *L'Homme qui rit*. Set in England in the late sixteenth and early seventeenth century, the novel traces the life of the protagonist Gwynplaine, who was disfigured as a child and bears a permanent grin, and his companions – the blind and virtuous Dea, the itinerant entertainer Ursus and Ursus's wolf Homo. The novel reveals that Gwynplaine is the son of a nobleman, abducted as a child, and sold by King James II to a band of wanderers who mutilate children and force them to work as beggars or carnival freaks.

1895
German cultural theorist Aby Warburg (1866–1929) undertakes a long American journey, meeting veteran anthropologists at the Smithsonian Institution and various sites significant to the Pueblo people, Native Americans in the Southwestern United States. In Cochiti, New Mexico, Warburg receives a cosmological drawing with a snake from a priest. Warburg was fascinated by the architecture, rituals, masks, and abstract painting of the Hopi. He also met Mennonite missionary and ethnographer Heinrich R. Voth, who shared his knowledge of Hopi religion.

Early 1900s
The sacred dances of George Ivanovich Gurdjieff (c.1866–1949), a mystic and spiritual philosopher, are a series of movements to awaken humans to a higher state of consciousness. According to Gurdjieff, humans are in a state of 'sleep' that limits our feelings and thoughts, which are closely connected to the automatism of our movements. He developed the idea of a 'Fourth Way' of integrating the body, mind and emotions, and his sacred dances are intended to preserve and transmit the

laws of the universe, as well as develop the inner person, enabling them to break free from their 'sleep'.

1914–17
The creature Odradek appears in Franz Kafka's (1883–1924) 'The Cares of a Family Man', published in his collection of short stories *A Country Doctor* (1918). Odradek seems to represent a useless object, similar to an entanglement of worn threads, yet possesses human-like traits. Kafka's description of Odradek is deliberately obscure, and many different interpretations have been offered. Philosopher Willi Goetschel (b.1958) has surveyed the perspectives on Odradek, as a critique of capitalism from the perspective of Marxist literary criticism to a surfacing of repressed emotional trauma from a Freudian viewpoint.

1916
Sophie Taeuber-Arp's (1889–1943) *Coupe Dada* is a black lacquered turned wood sculpture that resembles an inverted cup. The simplicity of the monochrome form reflects Taeuber-Arp's search for a harmonious balance of shape and colour. The sculpture is one of several turned wood objects she made between 1916 and 1918, at times in collaboration with dada artist and her future husband, Jean Arp (1886–1966). During this period, Taeuber-Arp was involved in the Zürich dada movement, designing puppets, costumes, and sets for performances, while also producing textile and graphic works that explored geometric abstraction.

1918
Sophie Taeuber-Arp produces another turned wood object, *Puderdose* (Powder Compact), painted dusty rose. Similar to *Coupe Dada*, its upper half resembles an inverted cup, though longer, and it stands on an inverted funnel.

1921
Aby Warburg is hospitalised in a neurological clinic in Kreuzlingen, Switzerland, apparently suffering from manic depression and showing signs of schizophrenia. His condition would improve while he was in the clinic, and on 21 April 1923, he would give a lecture about the Hopi and serpent rituals. The lecture was done to negotiate his discharge from the sanatorium: for the doctors, the test of sanity was an hour's talk. However, for Warburg, the lecture was also a means for him to revive the material on the Hopi and affirm the partnership of scholarly and personal resolution.

1922
Born out of the Bauhaus, Oskar Schlemmer's (1888–1943) *Triadic Ballet* is the most widely known avant-garde artistic dance piece. The ballet is anchored on the principle of the trinity, with three acts and three performers. Conceiving of the human body as a medium, Schlemmer designs costumes using cylinders, cones, spheres and spiral shapes to demonstrate his ideas of choreographed geometry. For Schlemmer, the ballet represents a synthesis of mechanised and primordial impulses, the currents propelling the modern world forward.

1956
The novel *The Roots of Heaven* by French writer and Second World War aviator Romain Gary (born Roman Kacew, 1914–80) is first published in French. Its protagonist Morel is a concentration camp survivor and an environmentalist who travels to French Equatorial Africa, leading a campaign to ban the killing of elephants. The novel would win the Lithuanian-born Gary his first Prix Goncourt. In 1975, he won the prize a second time for his novel of that year *The Life Before Us*, which was published under the name Émile Ajar, one of several pseudonyms he had adopted. The truth of Ajar's identity was eventually revealed in Gary's suicide note in 1980.

1961
Edward Norton Lorenz (1917–2008), the American mathematician and meteorologist, founds 'chaos theory', which has had a far-reaching influence on various branches of science. His visualisation of the unpredictability of future outcomes due to variable factors in the present is called a Lorenz Attractor, and its two-winged form would also come to represent what Lorenz described in later years as the 'butterfly effect'.

1965
American artist Sol LeWitt (1928–2007) creates the first sculptures of modular pieces of open cubic forms, which are shown in his solo exhibition at the Daniels Gallery in New York. The following year, LeWitt begins combining modular pieces in serial forms to generate various combinations. A prominent figure in the minimalism movement that emerged in New York in the 1960s, and also an early proponent of conceptual art, LeWitt wrote in 1967 in one of his seminal texts, 'Paragraphs on Conceptual Art' (published in the Summer 1967 issue of *Artforum*): 'In conceptual art the idea or concept is the most important aspect of the work. When an artist uses a conceptual form of art,

it means that all of the planning and decisions are made beforehand and the execution is a perfunctory affair.'

1968 (a)
Inspired by the frescoes he saw during his 1963 visit to the Great Tomb of Gangseo in North Korea, Isang Yun (1917–95) composes *Images* for flute, oboe, violin and violoncello, in the guarded hospital room to which he was transferred after a physical breakdown while imprisoned in what is known as the East Berlin Incident. On 17 June 1967, Yun was kidnapped from West Berlin by the South Korean secret service. He was taken to Seoul via Bonn, condemned for espionage, and threatened with life imprisonment by the government. Yun's visit to the Great Tomb of Gangseo was crucial in the charge against him for spying.

1968 (b)
The first full text-to-speech system developed by a group of researchers including Noriko Umeda at the Electrotechnical Laboratory in Japan is demonstrated. The developments in text-to-speech conversion are soon applied to electronic devices and consumer goods, including the Speak & Spell toy introduced in 1978 by Texas Instruments, Sun Electronics's arcade game *Stratovox* in 1980 and speech-generating devices to support people with speech impairments.

1987
Mass protests take place between 10 and 29 June during the June Struggle, a nationwide democracy movement in South Korea. The protests are triggered by the military regime's announcement of Roh Tae-woo as the next president, which protestors see as an affront to the process, already delayed, to revise the South Korean constitution to permit direct elections. The demonstrations eventually pushed the government to hold elections and introduce democratic reforms.

1988
Aby Warburg's *Schlangenritual: Ein Reisebericht* is published in Berlin, with a foreword by Ulrich Raulff. This German publication is a translation of the 1938 English publication 'A Lecture on Serpent Ritual', which was itself a translation of a reconstruction of the lecture based on Warburg's notes, and a renewed reconstruction of Warburg's notes. The travelogue traces Warburg's journey from his brother's New York wedding to New Mexico, detailing his observations of tribal rituals which included the use of the serpent as a symbol for lightning. The book delves into the relationship between fear and reason in the figure of the serpent, which is also present in Indian, Greek and Biblical mythology.

2000
The first version of Haegue Yang's *Grid Bloc* is published in A4 size. Through her frequent use of millimetre paper for her artistic practice, Yang discovered that certain colours or dimensions were not available in stationery shops. As a way to resist industrial standardisation, Yang's *Grid Bloc* contains different grid line intervals in various colours, inserting these 'unindustrialized norms' into the market. Yang will later expand the work to reflect and enable the development of her paper collage series *Trustworthies* 2010–ongoing, which are made of security patterns from the inside of envelopes on the backdrop of a collaged *Grid Bloc*.

2008
A Small Dictionary for Haegue Yang by Doryun Chong is commissioned in the framework of Yang's solo exhibition *Asymmetric Equality* at REDCAT, Los Angeles, and published in the eponymous catalogue edited by Clara Kim. It deals with twelve keywords, which include figures such as Hannah Arendt and Chris Marker, concepts such as community and hometown, and methodologies such as origami.

2011 (a)
Yang presents her first wallpaper piece, *Field of Teleportation*, at her solo show *The Art and Technique of Folding the Land*, Aspen Art Museum. The work was produced in collaboration with Berlin-based designer Manuel Raeder. Its zero gravity landscape functions as a backdrop to a microcosm of flattened works and installation views suspended in space. 'Shrinking the ground', an East Asian concept popularised in Taoist mythology of moving over long distances instantaneously, influenced Yang's reference to notions of movement, such as teleportation.

2011 (b)
Yang develops *Dress Vehicles*, a new series of blind installations comprising floor-based structures that can be entered into and moved around, for her solo exhibition *Teacher of Dance* at Modern Art Oxford. The works referenced the stereometric costumes of Schlemmer's *Triadic Ballet*, while the exhibition's title alluded to

G.I. Gurdjieff and his ideas regarding movement, which were instrumental in the formation of Yang's works.

2012

During a residency at the Singapore Tyler Print Institute (STPI), Yang develops several print and papermaking techniques using the colours and textures of local and regional herbs and spices to create *Spice Sheets* 2012 and *Spice Prints* 2012, among other works. These would go on to be shown at her 2013 solo show at STPI, *Honesty Printed on Modesty*. The humble spices were used to examine the weightier subject of Singapore and the region's colonial history, tracing the cultural and economic transformations brought about by migration.

2013(a)

A second lexicon by Chong, *A Less Small Dictionary (for HY)*, is published in the catalogue accompanying Yang's solo show *Family of Equivocations*, Aubette 1928 and Museum of Modern and Contemporary Art, Strasbourg. Aubette 1928 was decorated by Sophie Taeuber-Arp, Jean Arp and Theo van Doesburg. The works in the exhibition include mobile performative sculptures and a wallpaper that references the avant-garde artistic movements. A new series of *Sonicwear*, garments made from bells, pays homage to Taeuber-Arp's dada costumes, marking the first instance of the artist being referenced in Yang's works.

2013(b)

Yang participates in a three-month residency at the Glasgow Sculpture Studios, which she devotes to learning macramé. At her show, *Journal of Bouba/kiki*, Glasgow Sculpture Studios, her first macramé piece, *Floating Knowledge and Growing Craft – Silent Architecture Under Construction* 2013 is exhibited. It is accompanied by an iPod playing a selection of podcasts and audio files – including Hugo's *The Man Who Laughs*, which Yang listened to while making the work – to offer a glimpse of the time invested into the labour-intensive weaving process. The exhibition also includes *Glasgow Tales of Laugh* 2013, an installation comprising ten boards, featuring excerpts from *The Man Who Laughs* interspersed with plaster objects and black-and-white photographs taken by Yang as she wandered around the Necropolis and the Glasgow Botanic Gardens.

2013(c)

Boxing Ballet is conceived for Yang's exhibition *Journal of Echomimetic Motions*, Bergen Kunsthall. The exhibition space is transformed into a stage comprising mobile sculptures and wall pieces, acting as both scenic elements and active protagonists. The constellation of movable *Sonic Figures* – anthropomorphic and geometric sculptures covered in golden bells – demonstrates Yang's continued exploration of abstraction and movement in Schlemmer's *Triadic Ballet*, ideas that had already emerged in the *Dress Vehicles* developed in 2011.

2014

Yang rents a space as a studio in Seoul for the first time; it is still used as her Seoul studio today.

2015(a)

Yang's solo exhibition *Shooting the Elephant 象 Thinking the Elephant* is held at Leeum, Samsung Museum of Art, Seoul. The title is inspired by George Orwell's essay 'Shooting an Elephant' and Gary's *The Roots of Heaven*, and the elephant – a powerful yet vulnerable creature – serves as a metaphor for nature and human dignity. The exhibition introduces a new series of sculptures, *The Intermediates*; these architectural and anthropomorphic sculptures, made from woven synthetic straw, use techniques from traditional crafts considered 'folk' to address the particularity and universality of cultures, blurring the boundaries between established traditional concepts and hybrid migratory strands. *Hovering Lion Dance – Trustworthy #240* 2015, a new work from the *Trustworthies* series of collages, is presented for the first time as a large-scale wall piece.

2015(b)

Yang's solo exhibition *Come Shower or Shine, It Is Equally Blissful* at the Ullens Center for Contemporary Art, Beijing presents her major works, from 1994 to recent commissioned sculptural installations. The landscape of material hybridity – featuring spices, venetian blinds, clothing racks, synthetic straw, Choco Pies, bells and graph paper – demonstrates the plurality of Yang's unique visual language. A monumental work, *Virtuous Edibles – Affection and Benevolence* 2015 is conceived for the exhibition: comprising two towers, each weighing 500 kg, the sculpture is constructed from Choco Pie packages with the characters of 情 (affection) and 仁 (benevolence), delineating the respective product markets of Korea and China.

2015 (c)
Yang's first use of turbine vents, at *Sharjah Biennial 12: The past, the present, the possible*, Bait Al Aboudi, Sharjah. Yang's site-specific installation *An Opaque Wind* 2015 takes the intertwined geo-economic history of Korea in the Gulf region since the 1970s as a point of departure. The installation consists of a freestanding steel structure and various assemblages built from common construction elements including industrial vents that, like Sharjah's traditional towers, take advantage of directional winds. Yang would continue to use vents as a material to deal with non-materials like air and wind at her solo exhibition *An Opaque Wind Park in Six Folds* (2016), Serralves Museum of Contemporary Art, Porto. Here, the vents are integrated into her installation's towers to become glittering kinetic elements, a metaphor for migration and transitory encounters.

2016
Yang conceives a series of exhibitions with titles that start with *Quasi-Pagan*. The first is *Quasi-Pagan Minimal* at Greene Naftali, New York, followed by *Quasi-Pagan Serial* at Hamburger Kunsthalle, Hamburg, also 2016. The exhibitions tangentially address the clash between Yang's newly discovered interest in pagan culture and her struggle with the canon of modernity. Western art history, which is strongly anchored in the development of Christianity in Western Europe as a basis of many cultural and art shifts, is agony for Yang; pagan culture offers an alternative point of entry to Western culture.

2017 (a)
For *Ornament and Abstraction*, Yang's first solo exhibition at kurimanzutto, Mexico City, she brings in two references: the essay 'Ornament and Crime' (1913) by architect and theorist Adolf Loos (1870–1933) and pre-Columbian gold objects. The first enables Yang to reconsider ornamentation from today's point of view, attitudes having shifted and evolved drastically over the century since Loos published his essay. Yang resolutely brings weaving techniques into the realm of ornamentation, which has been demonised by the majority of advocators of modernism. The exhibition suggests that there is common ground between ornamentation and modernism and presents works where geometry and ornamentation meet in a mesmerising enchantment of mutating shapes and forms. Just as golden ritualistic objects such as the Muisca Raft in Muisca culture are sacred, Yang also sees a spiritual impulse in the drive towards mechanical expansion in modernism. Aby Warburg plays a role as a virtual reference. His 1923 lecture on the serpent ritual addresses the artificial categorisation of iconography into Western and non-Western scholarship and discusses how the serpent, which is perceived as a pagan symbol, appears across civilisations. Warburg's openness to go beyond a conventional reading of history and identify connections between cultures inspired Yang's attempt to bring ornamentation and modernism into dialogue with each other.

2017 (b)
Yang's third blind installation with motoric movements is presented in *Silo of Silence – Clicked Core* at KINDL – Centre for Contemporary Art, Berlin. (The two previous installations were *Approaching: Choreography Engineered in Never-Past Tense* 2012 at Documenta XIII in Kassel and *Three Folds and Multiple Twists* 2013, produced by and presented at Glasgow Sculpture Studios.) All three movements were equally motoric, and examples of the few times that Yang has broken away from her reluctance to make things physically move.

2018 (a)
Yang's *ETA 1994–2018* takes place at Museum Ludwig, Cologne. Consisting of approximately 120 works, it is regarded as Yang's first survey show and includes several reconstructions of her early pieces from 1994 and 1995. The presentation is not strictly chronological, though a rough timeline is maintained.

2018 (b)
For the first time, Yang uses speakers, arranged as 'sound fruit' and also serving as sound elements to glue the sculptures and their environment together, at *Beautiful world, where are you?*, Liverpool Biennial, Tate Liverpool. The installation includes a wallpaper piece, *Dockside Rock and Roll* (in collaboration with Mike Carney), which was based on initial research about the dualistic aspects of local history, including pagan culture – such as the maypole dance and spiritual stone sites – as well as the heavy rise and fall of historical local industries, such as shipbuilding and the slave trade.

2018 (c)
Yang collaborates again with Manuel Raeder to conceive another wallpaper, *Incubation and Exhaustion*. Their third collaboration is presented at her solo show *Chronotopic Traverses* at La Panacée-MO.CO, Montpellier.

2018(d)
Yang undertakes a field trip in several cities in Australia for *Superposition: Art of Equilibrium and Engagement*, Biennale of Sydney. This trip, which included visits to Alice Springs and Adelaide, was instrumental in Yang's understanding of aboriginal art, which is deeply connected with knowledge of life in relationship to the land. Her group of sculptures, *Umbra Creatures by Rockhole* 2017–18, was implanted in the show *Triple Vita Nestings* at the Institute of Modern Art, Brisbane, 2018 as well as at Govett-Brewster Art Gallery, New Plymouth, New Zealand. The idea of 'nesting' relates to the formal strategies Yang employed – such as layering, doubling, splitting and merging – to reveal how individual subjects are embedded in the lives, stories and contexts of others.

2019(a)
Yang presents a set of sound elements comprising twenty-six TTS (Text to Speech) recordings of the phrase 'the source of art is in the life of a people', which is installed at the centre of her solo show *Tracing Movement* at South London Gallery. Hidden beneath the gallery's wooden floor is an original marquetry panel, designed in 1891 by the English artist Walter Crane (1845–1915) and inscribed with this phrase, which Yang mobilised and transformed into artificial productions of human speech, highlighting its invisibility as a buried piece of history.

2019(b)
Yang's solo show *When The Year 2000 Comes* is her first exhibition at Kukje Gallery in Seoul. Multisensory elements of sound, fog, light and scents transform the gallery alongside sonic and mobile sculptures. A new series of *Sonic Gym Sculptures*, derived from *Sonic Sculptures* and suspended from the ceiling, generate patterns and acoustics when rotated. At the opening, face-painting sessions are held. The exhibition is accompanied by performances of Isang Yun's *Images* (1968), the flying of drone soccer balls, and lectures.

2019(c)
Yang's installation *Handles* opens at MoMA, New York. Commissioned for the Marron Atrium, the installation features six monumental sculptures mounted on castors and manoeuvred by means of handles. Steel grab bars are mounted on the walls amid an iridescent pattern. The shapes of the sculptures are inspired by Sophie Taeuber-Arp's *Coupe Dada* and *Puderdose*, the ideas of G.I. Gurdjieff, and open-source designs.

2019(d)
Yang presents the installation *Forum for Drone Speech – Singapore Simulations* at the National Gallery Singapore. The installation features a recording of Nadine, a humanoid social robot, reciting a script written by Yang in six languages (English, German, Hindi, Mandarin, Japanese and French). The combination of Yang's sculptures on a faux marble structure with hologram prints of images related to Singapore's history, alongside a recording of birdsong and Nadine's robotic voice, evokes an interplay of multiple realities.

2020
O2 & H2O, the title of Yang's solo exhibition at the National Museum of Modern and Contemporary Art, Korea, reappropriates *Air and Water*, the title of a 2002 artwork and exhibition, using chemical formulae rather than words and reflecting on the artist's own exhibition history. Noteworthy new works in this exhibition include the synthetic voice piece *Genuine Cloning* 2020 and two digital collages – the banner *Five Doing Un-Doing* 2020 and the wallpaper *DMZ Un-Do* 2020. Each of them adopts similar themes and interests around technology and modern civilisation, refracting them into disparate visual languages. Another new work, *Sonic Domesticus* 2020, reproduces and expands the dimensions of ordinary household items – an iron, a hair dryer, a pot-kettle and a computer mouse – to form an ensemble of four sculptures. Introduced as an 'exhibition-within-an-exhibition' – an unprecedented format in Yang's output – are 108 wooden spoons produced by the Mok Woo Workshop, raising questions concerning housekeeping, community and voice.

Extract taken from:
Doryun Chong, 'The Third Effort toward a Dictionary for Haegue Yang' in *Separating and Binding: A Collection of Writings on Haegue Yang, 2001–2020*, Seoul 2020.
Reproduced with the permission of the authors and the National Museum of Modern and Contemporary Art, Korea and Hyunsil Publishing, Seoul.

List of Exhibited Works
Gallery 5

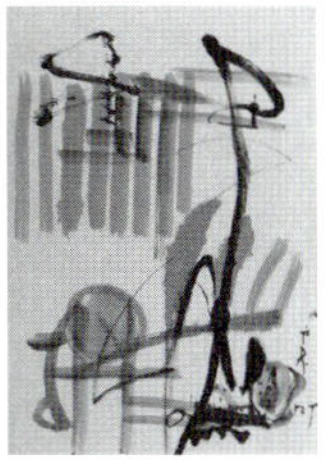

Li Yuan-chia
Untitled 1954–61
Ink and watercolour paint on paper
54.7 × 39.2 cm

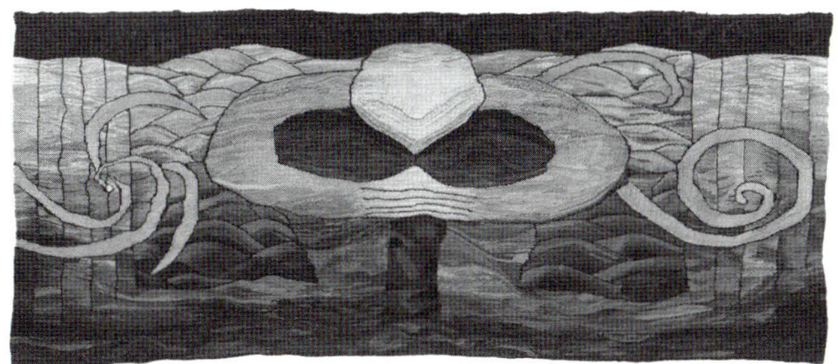

Li Yuan-chia
Untitled c.1980–2
Tapestry
101 × 240.2 cm

Li Yuan-chia
1+1=1-1 1965
Paint and fabric on canvas
50.2 × 60.2 cm

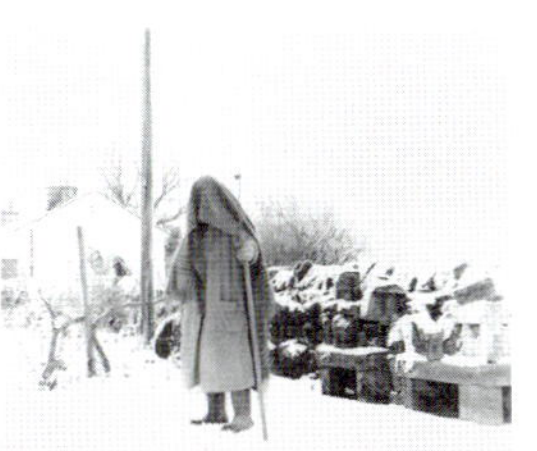

Li Yuan-chia
Untitled 1993
Photograph, hand-coloured black and white print on paper
19.6 × 23.2 cm

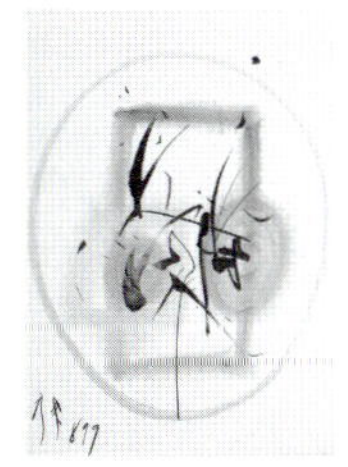

Li Yuan-chia
Untitled 1954–61
Ink and watercolour paint on paper
53.5 × 38.3 cm

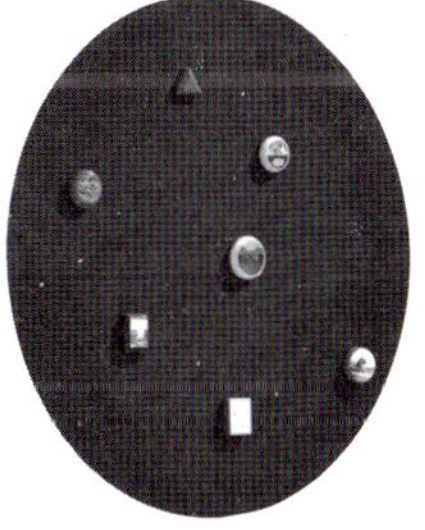

Li Yuan-chia
Untitled 1980s
Paint on metal, paint on wood with photographs and magnets
91.5 × 91.5 cm

Li Yuan-chia
1+1-1 1965
Paint and fabric on canvas
50.5 × 60.3 cm

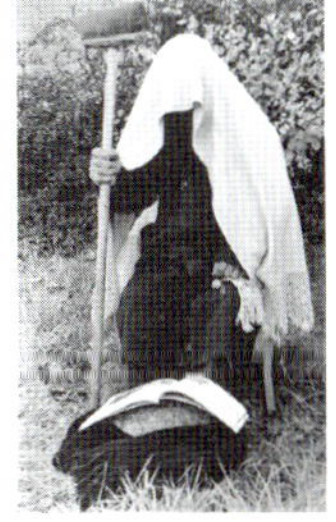

Li Yuan-chia
Untitled 1993
Photograph, hand-coloured black and white print on paper
40.5 × 25.3 cm

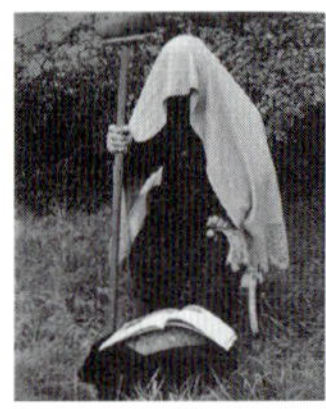

Li Yuan-chia
Untitled 1993
Photograph, hand-coloured black and white print on paper
24.6 × 20.5 cm

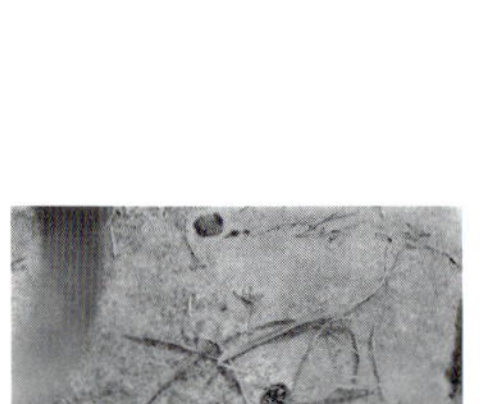

Li Yuan-chia
Untitled 1993
Photograph, hand-coloured black and white print on paper
18.8 × 23.4 cm

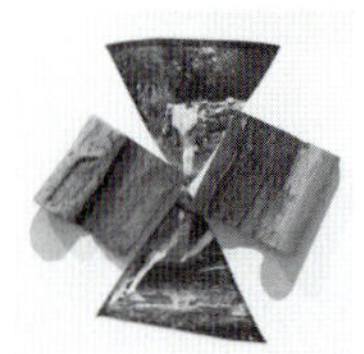

Li Yuan-chia
Untitled 1993–4
Paint, photographs and wood on board
63 × 61.8 cm

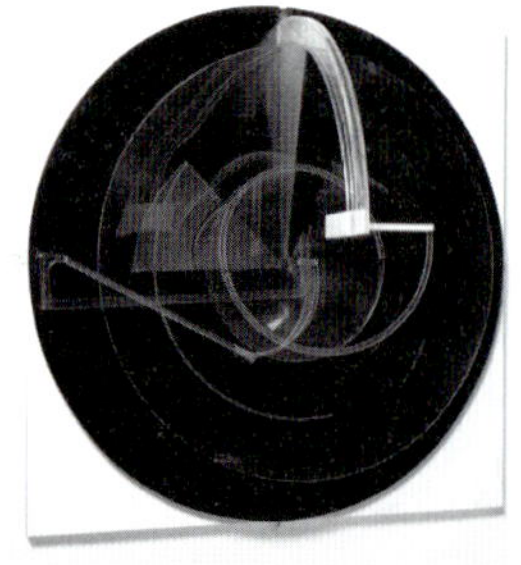

Naum Gabo
Circular Relief c.1925
Plastic on wood
49.8 × 49.8 × 22.9 cm
Tate. Presented by the artist 1977

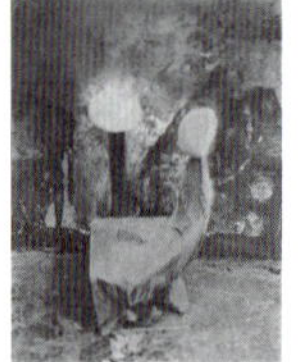

Li Yuan-chia
Untitled 1993
Photograph, hand-coloured black and white print on paper
41.5 × 30.7 cm

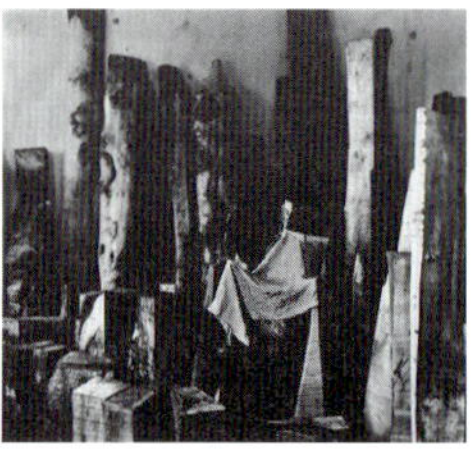

Li Yuan-chia
Untitled 1993
Photograph, hand-coloured black and white print on paper
20.4 × 23 cm

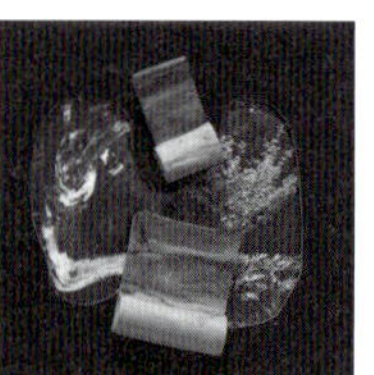

Li Yuan-chia
Untitled 1993–4
Paint, photographs and wood on board
64 × 63.5 cm

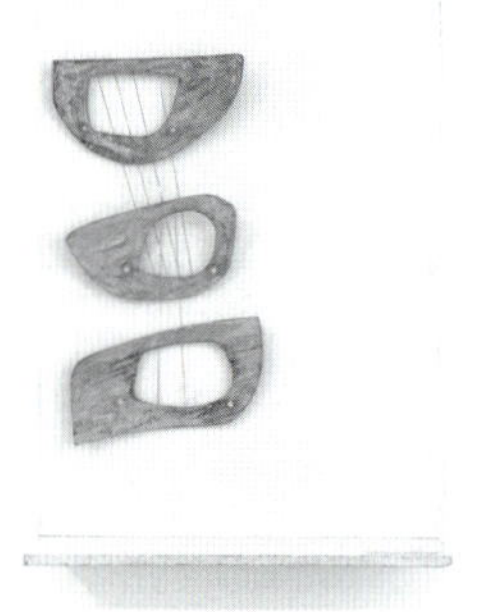

Dame Barbara Hepworth
Maquette, Three Forms in Echelon 1961
Brass and string on wooden board and shelf
67.2 × 50.3 × 21.8 cm
Tate. Presented by the executors of the artist's estate 1980

All works by Li Yuan-chia: Courtesy of the Li Yuan-chia Foundation

Gallery 6

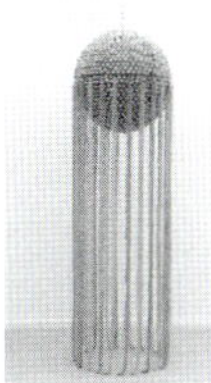

Sonic Half Moon Type II – Medium Light #17 2014
Powder-coated steel frame and mesh, steel wire rope, brass and nickel plated bells, metal rings
173 × 54 × 54 cm

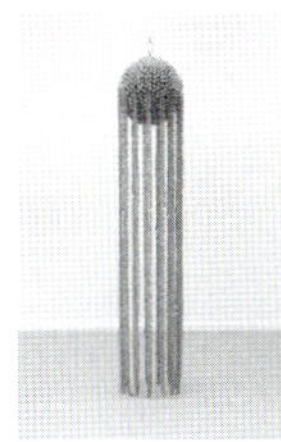

Sonic Half Moon Type III – Tiny Regular #7 2015
Powder-coated steel frame and mesh, steel wire rope, brass and nickel plated bells, metal rings
162 × 34 × 34 cm

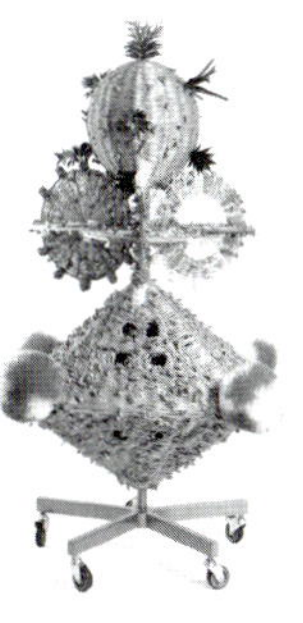

The Intermediate – Airflow of Pyramid Winnow 2015
Artificial straw, powder-coated steel frame, castors, plastic raffia string, artificial plants
180 × 95 × 95 cm
Courtesy of Galerie Barbara Wien, Berlin

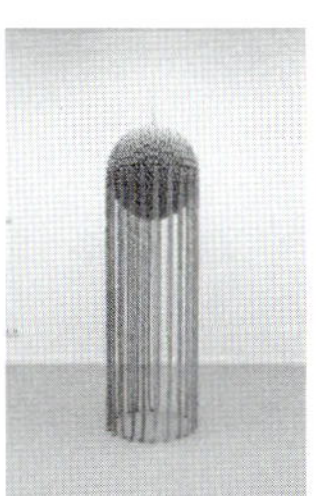

Sonic Half Moon Type IV – Medium Light #19 2014
Powder-coated steel frame and mesh, steel wire rope, brass and nickel plated bells, metal rings
173 × 54 × 54 cm

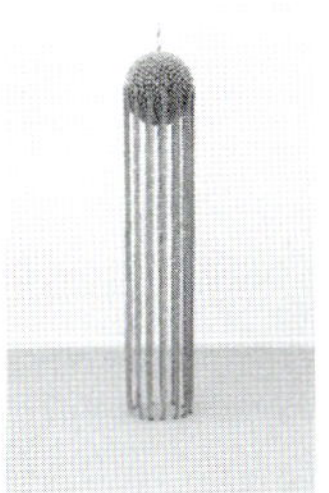

Sonic Half Moon Type IV – Tiny Regular #8 2015
Powder-coated steel frame and mesh, steel wire rope, brass and nickel plated bells, metal rings
162 × 34 × 34 cm

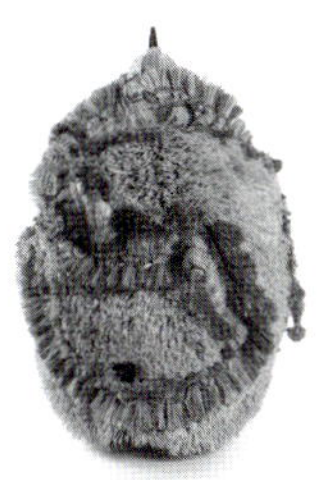

The Intermediate – Running Firecracker 2016
Artificial straw, powder-coated steel frame and mesh, castors, plastic raffia string, brass and copper plated bells
155 × 120 × 122 cm
Private collection, London

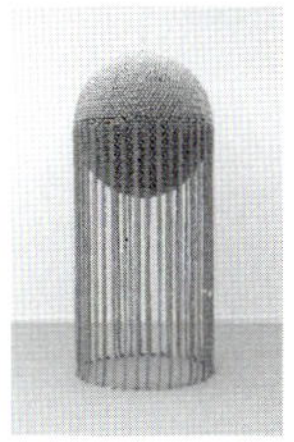

Sonic Half Moon Type II – Large Light #21 2014
Powder-coated steel frame and mesh, steel wire rope, brass and nickel plated bells, metal rings
187 × 84 × 84 cm

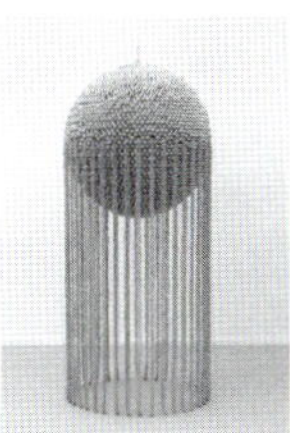

Sonic Half Moon Type III – Large Light #22 2015
Powder-coated steel frame and mesh, steel wire rope, brass and nickel plated bells, metal rings
187 × 84 × 84 cm

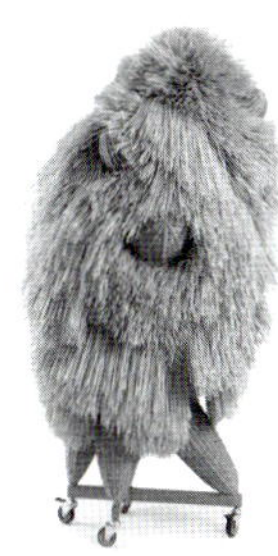

The Intermediate – Tilted Bushy Lumpy Bumpy 2016
Artificial straw, powder-coated steel frame and mesh, castors
203 × 120 × 120 cm
Marc and Annette Kemmler Collection

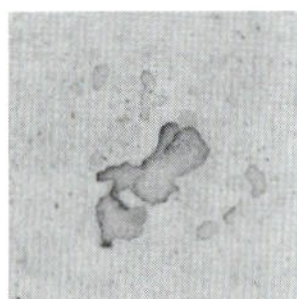

Afternoon Stain 2019
Chipboard, wood varnish, found plants, metal parts of clock, mesh produce bag parts, tea stain, dust, hair
30 × 30 × 2.2 cm

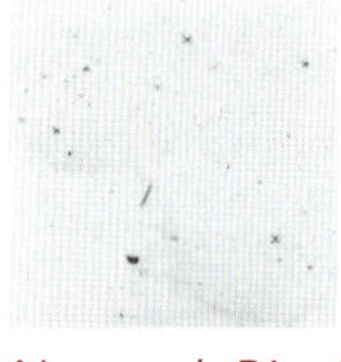

Network Bits 2019
Chipboard, wood varnish, seeds, mesh produce bag parts, dust, hair
20 × 20 × 2.3 cm

Crimped Shooting Star 2019
Chipboard, wood varnish, seeds, spring, washers, dust, hair
60 × 60 × 2.5 cm

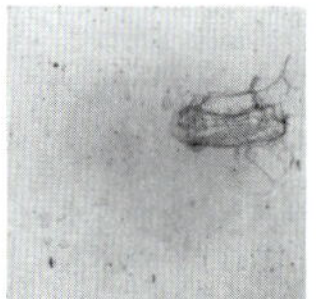

Small Deep Sea 2019
Chipboard, wood varnish, seeds, found plants, mesh produce bag part, tea stain, dust, hair
45 × 45 × 2.7 cm

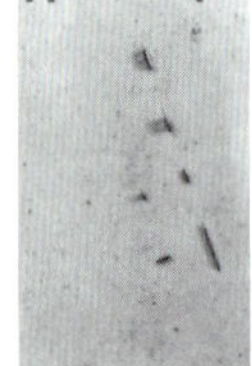

Blade Notations – Upstream Journey 2019
Chipboard, wood varnish, blades, seeds, dust, hair
56.2 × 35 × 4.2 cm

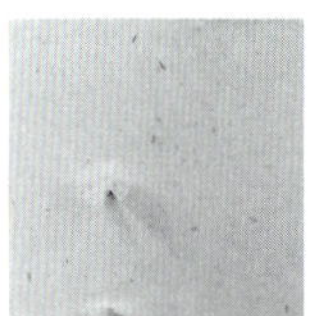

Parachuted Softly 2019
Chipboard, wood varnish, seeds, found plants, mesh produce bag, dust, hair
61.3 × 60 × 8.6 cm

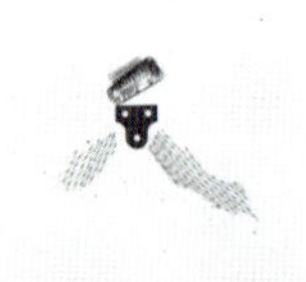

Mesh Mustache 2019
Chipboard, wood varnish, seeds, mesh produce bag parts, unknown metal parts, dust, hair
20 × 20 × 2.5 cm

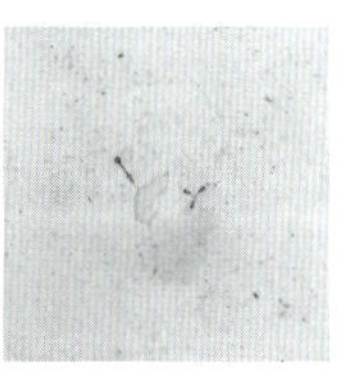
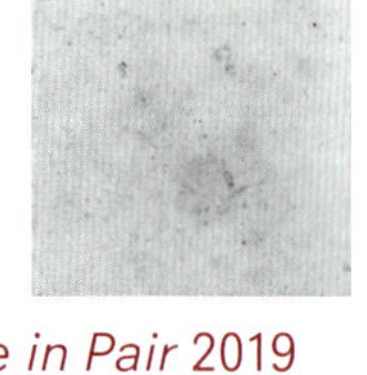

Stained Lapse in Pair 2019
Chipboard, wood varnish, seeds, clock hands, paper clip, sand, tea stain, dust, insect, hair
2 parts, each 45 × 45 × 2.2 cm

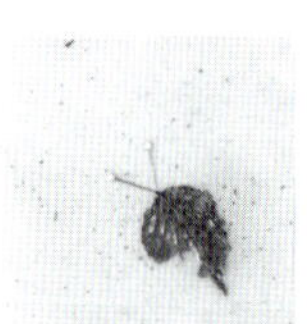

Pin-eyed Dead Leaf Butterfly 2019
Chipboard, wood varnish, seeds, found plant, pins, dust, hair
20 × 20 × 2.5 cm

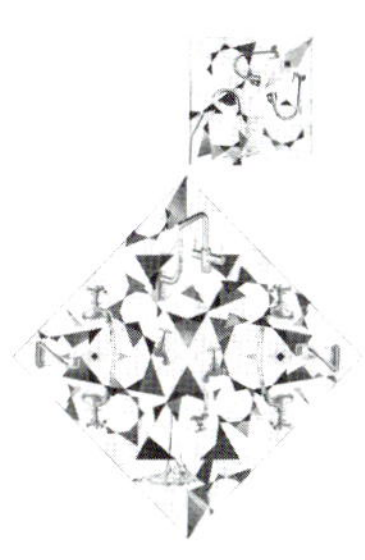

Fluidity on Nonagonal Crystal Matrix – Trustworthy #400 2020
Various security envelopes, graph paper, sandpaper, laser prints, self-adhesive holographic vinyl film on alu-dibond
2 parts, 86.2 × 86.2 cm; 43.2 × 43.2 cm
Courtesy of Galerie Chantal Crousel, Paris

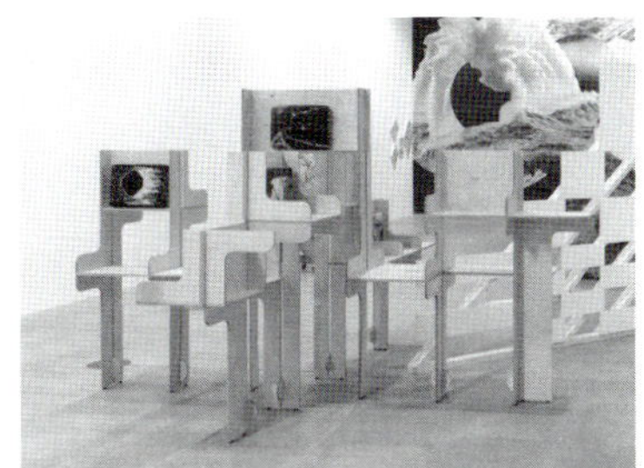

Mundus Cushion – Yielding X 2020
Clear-coated plywood, adjustable feet, screws, pegs, chip foam, canvas, knitting yarn, cotton yarn, jute twine
182 × 311 × 309 cm

Additional elements:

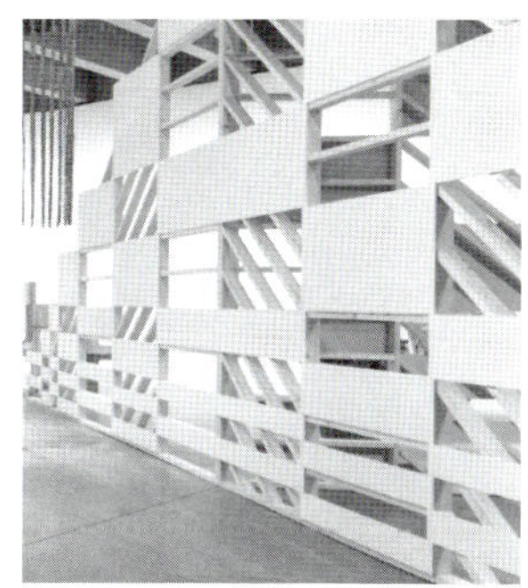

Shaped walls 2010–ongoing
Softwood, MDF, wood lath, wood glue, paint, screws
Dimensions variable

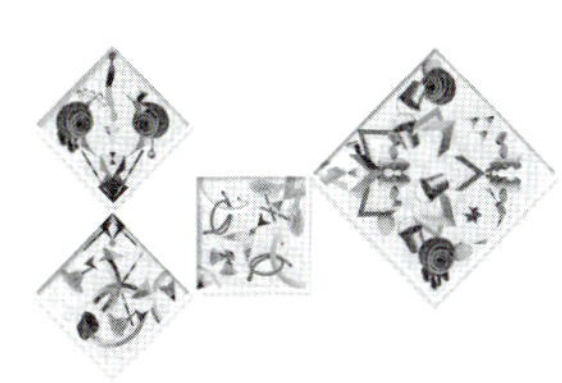

Cornish Healing Catch – Trustworthy #403 2020
Various security envelopes, graph paper, sandpaper, laser prints, self-adhesive holographic vinyl film on alu-dibond
4 parts, 57.2 × 57.2 cm; 36.2 × 36.2 cm

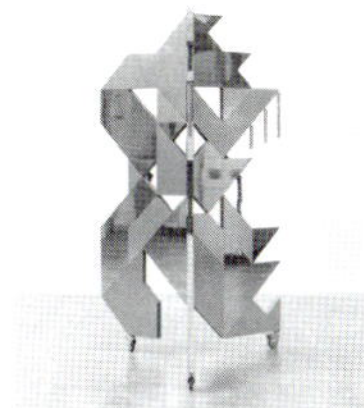

Reflected Metallic Cubist Dancing Mask 2020
Cherrywood, steel, ash wood handles, castors, self-adhesive glitter, holographic carbon and metal effect vinyl film, brass and nickel plated bells, metal rings
208 × 118 × 104 cm
Courtesy of Galerie Chantal Crousel, Paris

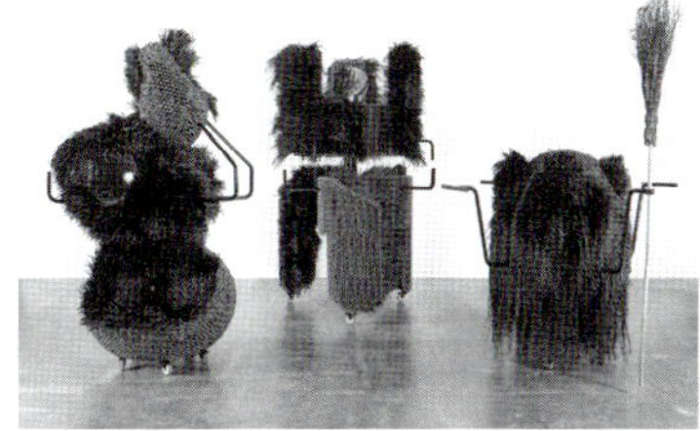

Sonic Intermediates – Three Differential Equations 2020
Powder-coated steel frame, mesh and handles, castors, turbine vent, brass, copper and nickel plated bells, metal rings, plastic twine, broom
Sonic Intermediate – Parameters and Unknowns after Li
215 × 172 × 172 cm
Sonic Intermediate – Parameters and Unknowns after Hepworth
216 × 125 × 125 cm
Sonic Intermediate – Parameters and Unknowns after Gabo
220 × 145 × 145 cm
Courtesy of Galerie Barbara Wien, Berlin

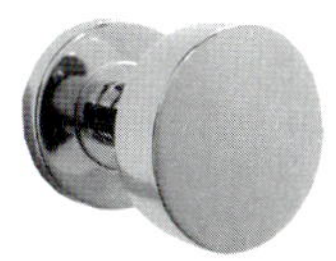

Handles on the wall 2019–ongoing
Plated steel handles
Dimensions variable

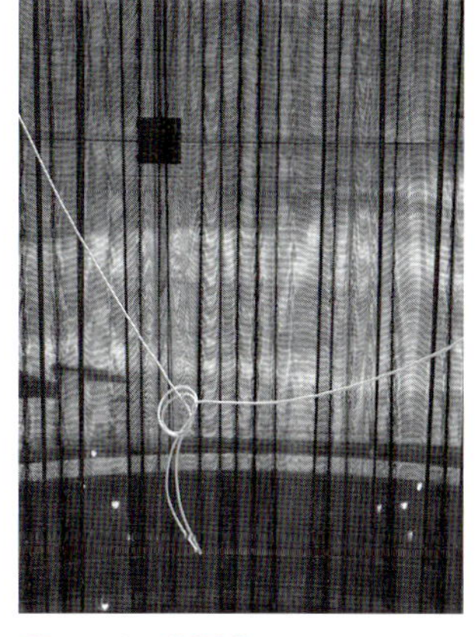

Curtain 2020
Fabric
Dimensions variable
Supported by Kvadrat

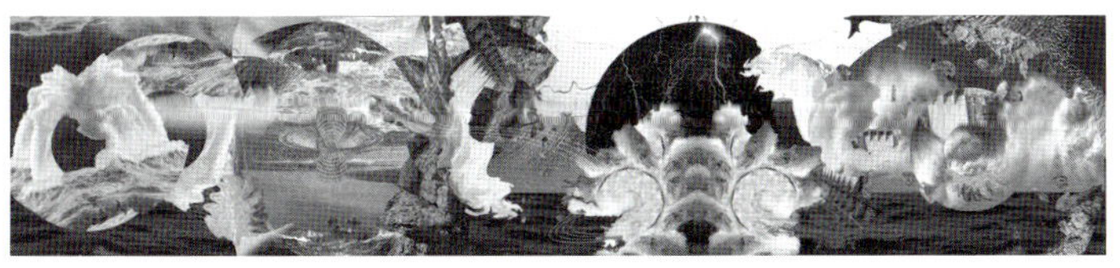

Non-Linear and Non-Periodic Dynamics 2020
Digital print on self-adhesive vinyl film
Dimensions variable

Gallery 8

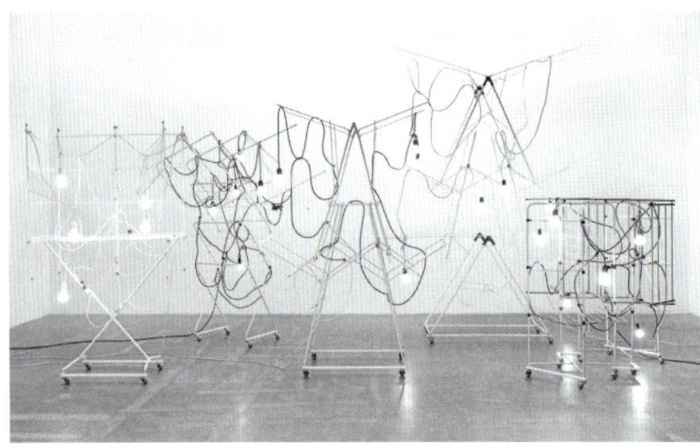

Non-Indépliables, nues 2010/2020
Drying racks, castors, light bulbs, cable, zip ties, terminal strips
Non-Indépliable, nue – Crowny Figure in Crossed Leg
183 × 105 × 78 cm
Non-Indépliable, nue – Lifting Up
191 × 140 × 75 cm
Non-Indépliable, nue – Sandwich Swing Squeezed Between Buildings
129 × 156 × 108 cm
Non-Indépliable, nue – Three Hearts Lifts a Sprout
198 × 144 × 62 cm
Non-Indépliable, nue – Three Times on Shoulder
264 × 188 × 62 cm

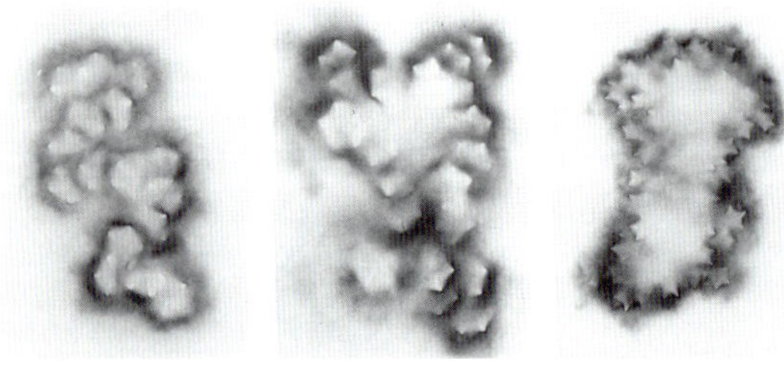

Non-Folding – Geometric Tipping #73 2015
Non-Folding – Geometric Tipping #77 2015
Non-Folding – Geometric Tipping #78 2015
Spray paint on paper
100 × 72 cm

All works courtesy of the artist, unless otherwise specified

Image Credits

Biographies

Haegue Yang (b. 1971) lives and works in Berlin and Seoul. She is Professor of Fine Arts at the Staedelschule in Frankfurt am Main. Yang has participated in major international exhibitions including the 16th Istanbul Biennial (2019); the 21st Biennale of Sydney (2018); La Biennale de Montréal (2016); the 12th Sharjah Biennial (2015); the 9th Taipei Biennial (2014); Documenta XIII in Kassel (2012); and the 53rd Venice Biennale (2009) as the South Korean representative as well as in the International Art Exhibition at the Arsenale. Recipient of the 2018 Wolfgang Hahn Prize, she held a survey exhibition titled *ETA* at the Museum Ludwig in Cologne in the same year, which displayed over 120 works from 1994–2018.

Her current and recent solo exhibitions include *The Cone of Concern*, Museum of Contemporary Art and Design, Manila (2020–1); *O2 & H2O*, National Museum of Modern and Contemporary Art, Korea (2020–1); *Emergence*, Art Gallery of Ontario, Toronto (2020–1); *In the Cone of Uncertainty*, The Bass, Miami Beach (2019–20); *Handles*, Museum of Modern Art, New York (2019–21); and *Tracing Movement*, South London Gallery (2019).

Yang's work is included in permanent collections such as the Art Gallery of Ontario, Toronto; Centre Pompidou, Paris; Museum of Modern Art, New York; M+, Hong Kong; Tate, London; The Solomon R. Guggenheim Museum, New York; Remai Modern, Saskatoon; The Bass, Miami Beach; and The Walker Art Center, Minneapolis. Her work has been the subject of numerous monographs, such as *In the Cone of Uncertainty* (2019); *Anthology 2006–2018: Tightrope Walking and Its Wordless Shadow* (2019); *ETA 1994–2018* (2018); *VIP's Union* (2017); and *Family of Equivocations* (2013).

Anne Barlow is Director of Tate St Ives and the curator of *Haegue Yang: Strange Attactors* (2020–1). Previously, she was Director of Art in General, New York (2007–16), Curator of Education and Media Programs at the New Museum, New York (1999–2006) and Curator of Contemporary Art and Design at Glasgow Museums (1994–9). She was curator of the 5th Bucharest Biennale (2012), co-curator of the Latvian Pavilion at the 55th Venice Biennale (2013), and guest project curator for *The Jerusalem Show VII* (2014) and the 2nd Tbilisi Triennial, Georgia (2015).

Doryun Chong is Deputy Director, Curatorial and Chief Curator of M+, a new museum of visual culture that opens its Herzog & de Meuron-designed building in Hong Kong in 2020. Appointed as the inaugural Chief Curator in 2013, Chong oversees all curatorial activities and programmes encompassing the museum's three main disciplinary areas of design and architecture, moving image and visual art. Prior to joining M+, he worked in various curatorial capacities at the Museum of Modern Art, New York (2009–13) and the Walker Art Center, Minneapolis (2003–9).

Magdalen Chua is an artist currently living in Warsaw. Her recent projects include *February Skies* at Proza, Wrocław (2019) and curating the two-part exhibition *Sandstorm in an Hourglass* in Singapore (2020). She has been working with Studio Haegue Yang as a copy-editor since 2014.

Hammad Nasar is presently co-curator of *British Art Show 9* (opening 2021) and is a Senior Research Fellow at the Paul Mellon Centre for Studies in British Art, where he co-leads the *London, Asia* research project and has collaboratively shaped programmes including a symposium on The LYC Museum & Art Gallery. Earlier, he was the inaugural Executive Director of the Stuart Hall Foundation, London (2018–19); Head of Research & Programmes at Asia Art Archive, Hong Kong (2012–16); and co-founder of the non-profit London art space, Green Cardamom (2004–12).

Studio Manuel Raeder is an interdisciplinary design studio based in Berlin, founded by Manuel Raeder in 2003. They create work in a wide range of formats exploring the boundaries between exhibitions, ephemera, books, type design, editing, publishing and furniture design, approaching their designs as carriers of information, or experimental devices to document or conceive narratives.

Colophon

First published 2020 by order of the Tate Trustees by Tate St Ives in association with Tate Publishing, a division of Tate Enterprises Ltd, Millbank, London SW1P 4RG www.tate.org.uk/publishing to support the development of the exhibition:

HAEGUE YANG:
STRANGE ATTRACTORS
Tate St Ives, 24 October 2020–3 May 2021

Curated by Anne Barlow, Director of Tate St Ives, with Assistant Curator Giles Jackson

Supported by Henry Moore Foundation and Institut für Auslandsbeziehungen. With additional support from Kvadrat, Tate Members and Tate St Ives Members.

Publication edited by Anne Barlow and Giles Jackson
Texts by Anne Barlow, Doryun Chong, Magdalen Chua and Hammad Nasar
Copy-edited by Neil Stewart
Designed by Studio Manuel Raeder
(Lucas Liccini and Manuel Raeder)
Printed by Benedict Press

A catalogue record for this book is available from the British Library.

ISBN 978-1-84976-737-8

Acknowledgements

Exhibition Lenders
Galerie Barbara Wien, Berlin
Galerie Chantal Crousel, Paris
Annette and Marc Kemmler
Li Yuan-chia Foundation
Haegue Yang

Special thanks to
Galerie Barbara Wien
Galerie Chantal Crousel
Greene Naftali
Kukje Gallery
kurimanzutto
Magdalen Chua
interzone, Berlin
South into North

Studio Haegue Yang, Berlin
Sofia Duchovny, Atsushi Fukunaga, Liene Harms, John Matthew Heard, Atsuko Ichikawa, Chieko Idetsuki, Cheongjin Keem, Bokyung Kim, Zarah Landes, Nicolas Pelzer, Katharina Schwerendt, Emmy Skensved, Christopher Wierling

Studio Haegue Yang, Seoul
Hwiwon Chun, Hanna Hong, U-jung Jang, Hyesook Jung, Myoungjung Kim, Jeesu Lee, Sihyun Ryu, Solkyu Yang, Heejung Ye, Yena Yoo

Tate St Ives would also like to thank HM Government for providing Government Indemnity for the exhibition at Tate St Ives, and the Department for Digital, Culture, Media and Sport and Arts Council England for arranging the indemnity.

Enormous thanks go to Giles Jackson, Sally Noall, Helen Bent, Sara Matson and all other Tate St Ives staff members, technicians, artist educators and volunteers, as well as the Tate Conservation and Registrarial teams in London.

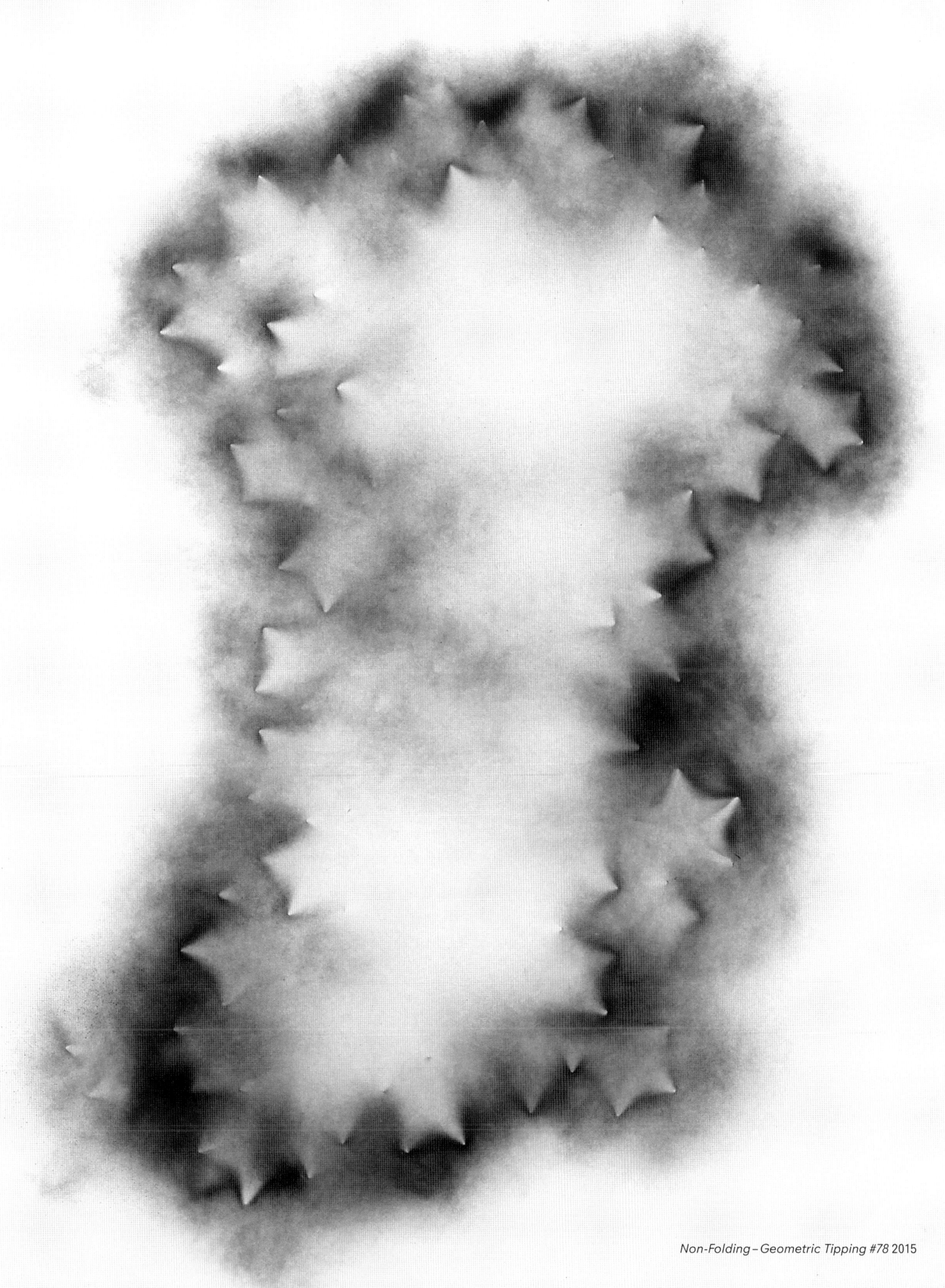

Non-Folding – Geometric Tipping #78 2015

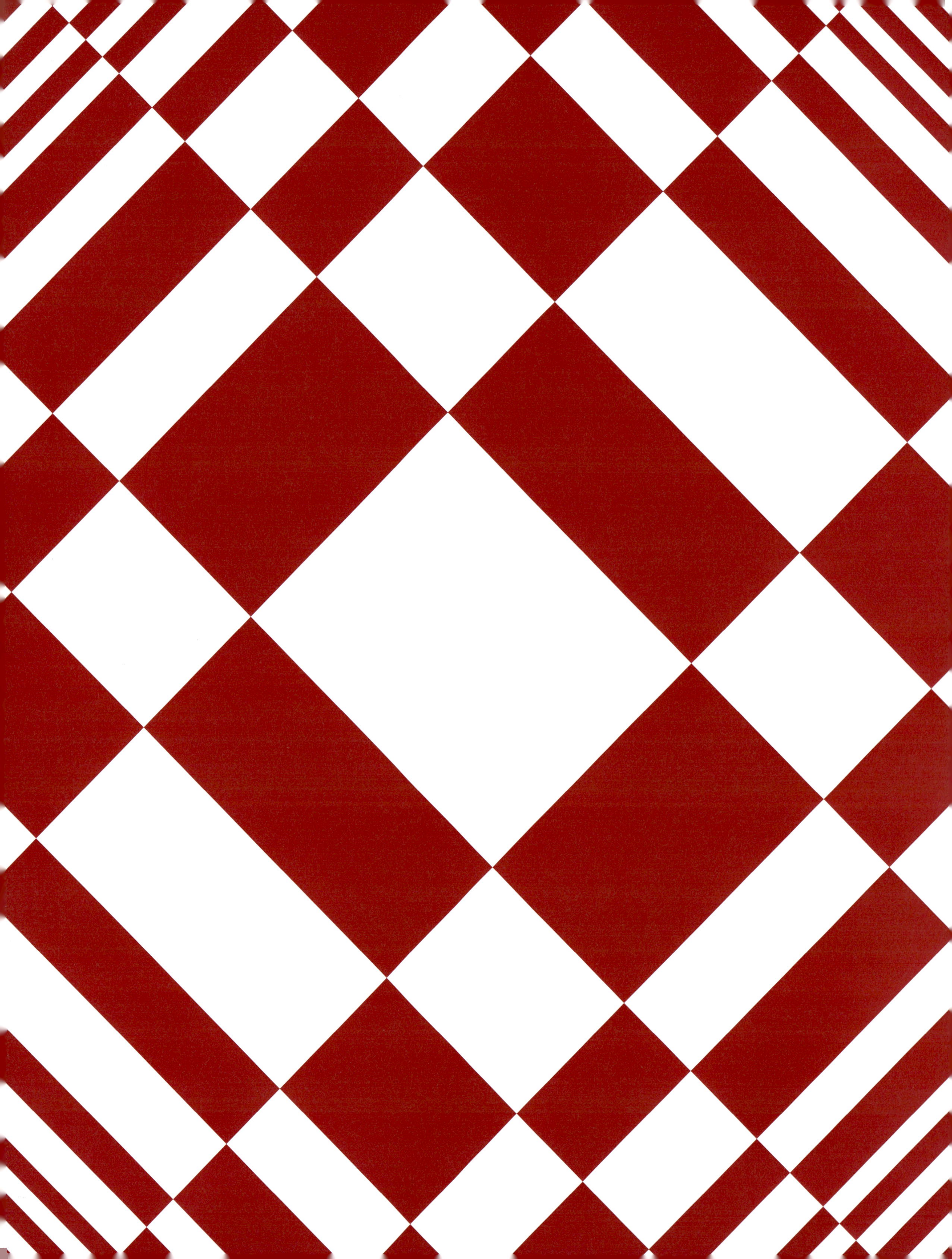